松涛館流空手道形教範全集
KATA GUIDE BOOK FOR ALL JAPAN KARATEDO SHOTOKAN

得意形 III TOKUI KATA III
鉄騎二段・鉄騎三段・半月・十手・珍手

Tekki Nidan / Tekki Sandan / Hangetsu / Jitte / Chinte

鉄騎二段 　　　鉄騎三段 　　　半月
Tekki Nidan　*Tekki Sandan*　*Hangetsu*

十手 　　　珍手
Jitte　*Chinte*

 一般財団法人全日本空手道松涛館

はじめに

Introduction

　空手道が武道・スポーツとして生涯を通じて全世界の人々に愛好され、オリンピック種目となるまでに普及・発展したことは誠に喜ばしい限りです。空手道が発展したのは、格闘技としての組手だけでなく、攻防の場面を仮想する形の両方が技術体系にあるからです。特に形には武道としての空手道の技が包含され、生涯を通じて修練をすることができます。

　松涛館流の空手道は船越義珍先生を始祖としますが、指導者から指導者へと伝わる中で時代の流れとともに技術が継承される過程で形も微妙に変化しています。世界には多くの松涛館流空手道の愛好者がいますが、このことは一層顕著に現れています。このような現状を踏まえ、松涛館流空手道の技術を普及・継承する団体として松涛館流の形についての教範を刊行し、競技会や段審査における形の評価に資することにしました。２０１６（平成２８）年の『松涛館流空手道形教範全集　基本形』に始まり、『松涛館流空手道形教範　得意形Ⅰ』、『松涛館流空手道形教範　得意形Ⅱ』を刊行し、この度は『松涛館流空手道形教範　得意形Ⅲ』を刊行する運びとなりました。

　得意形の第Ⅲ巻では、「鉄騎二段、鉄騎三段、半月、十手、珍手」を取り上げています。これらの形の中には公式競技会においてほとんど演武されることがない形もあります。形の特徴としては、鉄騎二段及び鉄騎三段は横一文字の演武線、半月は呼吸法と足の運び、十手は棒に対する攻防の技、珍手は特色ある開手技や手技です。いずれも松涛館流空手道を研究するのに適した形といえますので、形に習熟し、実際の場面を想定して応用技に熟達し、護身や健康、精神修養に活かしていただくことを期待しています。

　加盟団体をはじめ関係者においてはそれぞれの団体で受け継がれた伝統は大切にしながら、競技会や審査会等においてはこの教範を活用いただき、本法人の得意形についての理解を深め、充実した指導や稽古に活かしていただきたいと願っています。なお、この教範の写真と解説ですべてを伝えることには限界がありますので、本法人の講習会等でさら細部にわたって研究をしていただくようお願いします。

　本書の発行がさらなる空手道の発展につながることを祈念いたします。

2024（令和６）年８月
一般財団法人　全日本空手道松涛館中央技術委員会

　It is gratifying to see that karatedo is loved by people globally as a lifetime endeavor as a budo and as a sport. Karatedo has grown and is now being promoted as a part of the Olympic Games. The reason for karatedo's development is due to the fact that it has both kumite, as real combat, and kata, as an imaginary fight, in its training regime. In particular, kata contains all of the techniques of karatedo as a budo and can be practiced throughout one's life.

　The founder of Shotokan-ryu is Master Gichin Funakoshi. However, the kata of the style have changed subtly in the passage of time with the transmission from teacher to student. There are many Shotokan karatedo enthusiasts around the world, but this fact is very obvious. Considering this situation, we, the members of the Central Technical Committee, have published an instruction manual of Shotokan kata as an organization that disseminates the inherited the techniques of Shotokan-ryu. We believe that our work has contributed to the evaluation of Shotokan kata at tournaments and at examinations. Starting with Kata Guide Book for all Japan Karatedo Shotokan Kihon Kata in 2016, Kata Guide Book for all Japan Karatedo Shotokan Tokui Kata I and Kata Guide Book for all Japan Karatedo Shotokan Tokui Kata II have been published, and now we are pleased to announce the publication of Kata Guide Book for all Japan Karatedo Shotokan Tokui Kata III.

　Tokui Kata III features "Tekki Nidan, Tekki Sandan, Hangetsu, Jitte and Chinte. Some of these kata are rarely performed in official competitions. The kata are characterized by Tekki Nidan and Tekki Sandan as horizontal lines, Hangetsu as breathing and footwork, Jitte as offensive and defensive techniques against Bo and Chinte as distinctive open hand and hand techniques. All of these kata are suitable for the study of Shotokan-ryu karatedo, and we hope that you will become proficient in the kata and apply them to real combat situations for self-defense, health, and mental training.

　We hope that other member organizations and others concerned will use this instructor's manual at competitions and judging sessions to deepen their understanding of the kata in which our organization excels, and to apply it to their own training and instruction. Since there is a limit to what can be conveyed in the photos and explanations in this instructor's manual, we ask that you study the kata in more detail at our workshops and other events.

　We hope that the publication of this book will lead to the further development of karatedo.

September 2024 (Reiwa 6)
All Japan Karatedo Shotokan Central Technical Commitee

本書の活用にあたって
Regarding the use of this book

　一般財団法人全日本空手道松涛館は公益財団法人全日本空手道連盟（以下「全空連」という。）が制定している技術用語を使用することにしています。たとえば松濤館流の外受けを内受けに、内受けを外受けに表記しておりますことを承知願います。

　All Japan Karatedo Shotokan uses the technical terms established by the Japan Karatedo Federation (JKF).
　In particular, please note that Soto-Uke in Shotokan-ryu is written as Uchi-Uke, and Uchi-Uke is written as Soto-Uke.

【参考文献】
一般財団法人全日本空手道松涛館『松涛館流空手道形教範全集　基本形』(2016.4.28)
一般財団法人全日本空手道松涛館『松涛館流空手道形教範全集　得意形Ⅰ』(2018.7.30)
一般財団法人全日本空手道松涛館『松涛館流空手道形教範全集　得意形Ⅱ』(2020.8.28)
公益財団法人全日本空手道連盟『空手道形教範　第1指定形』(2017.10.19 改訂版)
公益財団法人全日本空手道連盟『空手道形教範　第2指定形』(2013.12.17)
公益財団法人全日本空手道連盟『空手道教範』(2015.3 改訂版)

もくじ
Contents

鉄騎二段　Tekki Nidan ･･････････････ 7
　挙動一覧 ･･････････････････････ 8
　各挙動解説 ････････････････････ 12

鉄騎三段　Tekki Sandan ･･････････････ 25
　挙動一覧 ･･････････････････････ 26
　各挙動解説 ････････････････････ 30

半月　Hangetsu ･･････････････････ 47
　挙動一覧 ･･････････････････････ 48
　各挙動解説 ････････････････････ 54

十手　Jitte ･･････････････････････ 73
　挙動一覧 ･･････････････････････ 74
　各挙動解説 ････････････････････ 78

珍手　Chinte ････････････････････ 91
　挙動一覧 ･･････････････････････ 92
　各挙動解説 ････････････････････ 98

（一財）全日本空手道松涛館のあゆみ

■ 2014 年 6 月 6 日
　「一般財団法人全日本空手道松涛館」を設立・登記

■ 2014 年 6 月 7 日
　公益財団法人全日本空手道連盟の評議員会において協力団体として承認

■ 2014 年 9 月 22 日
　（一財）全日本空手道松涛館　設立記念祝賀会開催（於　東京都・浅草ビューホテル）

■ 2015 年 7 月 12 日
　（一財）全日本空手道松涛館　第 1 回全国空手道選手権大会開催（於　東京都・日本武道館）

■ 2015 年 12 月 27 日
　全 9 地区協議会設立完了

■ 2016 年 4 月
　（一財）全日本空手道松涛館　『松涛館流空手道形教範全集　基本形』　発刊

■ 2018 年 7 月
　（一財）全日本空手道松涛館　『松涛館流空手道形教範全集　得意形Ⅰ』　発刊

■ 2020 年 8 月
　（一財）全日本空手道松涛館　『松涛館流空手道形教範全集　得意形Ⅱ』　発刊

■ 2024 年 9 月
　（一財）全日本空手道松涛館　『松涛館流空手道形教範全集　得意形Ⅲ』　発刊

■ 2024 年 9 月
　（一財）全日本空手道松涛館　創立 10 周年記念祝賀会開催（於　東京都・浅草ビューホテル）

■ 2024 年 9 月
　（一財）全日本空手道松涛館　第 10 回記念全国空手道選手権大会開催（於　東京都・日本武道館）

鉄騎二段
Tekki Nidan
（24 挙動）

首里手の拳聖といわれた糸洲安恒先生が鉄騎初段を参考に体育上の鍛練形として創作されたといわれている。鉄騎は旧名をナイファンチといい、鉄騎初段と同じ横一文字の演武線である。この形では正確な騎馬立ちのもとで中段のつかみ受けと掛け受けの区別を意識して体得しなければならない。

It is said that Anko Itosu sensei, the grand master of Shuri-te, created it as a kata for physical training based on Tekki Shodan. Tekki, formerly known as Naihanchi, is a single horizontal line of demonstration similar to that of Tekki Shodan. In this kata, one must be aware of the distinction between Tsukami-Uke and Kake-Uke in chudan under the correct Kibadachi.

鉄騎二段　挙動一覧

挙動23	挙動24-1	挙動24-2	止め

㊲	㊳	㊴	㊵

鉄騎二段　各挙動解説

直立	礼	直立	用意

①
【手の動作】
両手は開いて大腿部両側につけて伸ばす。

【足の動作】
結び立ち（左右とも正面に対して約30度）。

②
礼をする。

③
【手の動作】
手はそのまま。

【足の動作】
立ち方はそのまま。

④
【手の動作】
両拳を大腿部前にもっていく。

【足の動作】
左足、右足の順に開いて八字立ち。

【Hands】
Open both hands and extend them down along the sides of the thighs.

【Feet】
Musubidachi (left and right feet are angled approximately 30 degrees from the front).

* Bow (Rei).

【Hands】
Same as in ❶.

【Feet】
Same as in ❶.

【Hands】
Place both fists in front of the thighs.

【Feet】
From a Musubidachi, move the left foot, then right foot, out into a Hachijidachi.

* Explanation of terms in the text.
  Kou : The back of the hand
  Hira : The palm of the hand

| 挙動1 | 途中 | 挙動2 | 挙動3 |

【手の動作】
両肘を水平に張り、両拳（甲上向き）は胸前に構える。

【足の動作】
左足を前に交差する。

【留意点】
顔は西を向く。
顔、手、足をゆっくり揃える。

【手の動作】
両拳を顔の前で合わせる（両拳甲前向き）。

【足の動作】
右膝を右胸前にかい込む。

【手の動作】
右前腕右側面中段受け。左前腕胸前水平構え。

【足の動作】
右足を西へ強く踏み込み、騎馬立ち。

【手の動作】
右前腕正面下段受け（甲下向き）。左掌は虎口（親指と人差し指の間）を開き、右肘をはさむように添える。

【足の動作】
右足はそのままにして、左足を前に交差する。

【留意点】顔はそのまま。

【Hands】
Both arms bent, forearms in a straight line, both fists (Both Kou are up) kept in front of the chest.

【Feet】
Cross the left foot in front of the right foot.

【Note】
Turn the face to the west.
Simultaneously move the hands, feet and face slowly.

【Hands】
Bring both forearms together and both fists in front of the face (Both Kou are forward).

【Feet】
Pull the right knee up in front of the right chest.

【Hands】
Execute a Chudan-Uke to the right side with the right forearm. The left forearm is held horizontally in front of the chest (Kou is up).

【Feet】
Strongly step the right foot to the west into a Kibadachi.

【Hands】
Execute a Gedan-Uke in front with the right forearm (Kou is down). With the left hand, open the Ko-kou (thumb and fingers in the shape of a tiger's mouth) and place the right elbow on the Ko-kou as if biting it.

【Feet】
Keeping the right leg in place, cross the left foot in front of the right foot.

【Note】
The face is still keeping west.

挙動4	途中	挙動5	途中

⑨	⑩	⑪	⑫

【手の動作】
右前腕右側面下段受け（甲下向き）。左掌は右肘に添えたまま。

【足の動作】
右足を西へすり出し騎馬立ち。

【手の動作】
両肘を折り曲げ水平に張る。

【足の動作】
左足を引き寄せる。

【留意点】
顔を東へ向けながら、顔、手、足をゆっくり揃える。

【手の動作】
両肘を水平に張り、両拳（甲上向き）は胸前に構える。

【足の動作】
閉足立ち。

【手の動作】
両拳を顔の前で合わせる（両拳甲前向き）。

【足の動作】
左膝を左胸前にかい込む。

【Hands】
Execute a Gedan-Uke to the right side with the right forearm (Kou is down). The left palm remains attached to the right elbow.

【Feet】
Slide the right foot out to the west into a Kibadachi.

【Hands】
Bend both arms and lift both elbows.

【Feet】
Pull in the left leg.

【Note】
Turn the face to the east. Simultaneously move the hands, feet and face slowly.

【Hands】
Both arms bent, forearms in a straight line, both fists (Both Kou are up) kept in front of the chest.

【Feet】
Heisokudachi

【Hands】
Bring both forearms together and both fists in front of the face (Both Kou are forward).

【Feet】
Pull the left knee up in front of the left chest.

挙動6	挙動7	挙動8	挙動9

拡大

【手の動作】
左前腕左側面中段受け。右前腕胸前水平構え。

【足の動作】
左足を東へ強く踏み込み、騎馬立ち。

【手の動作】
左前腕正面下段受け（甲下向き）。右掌は虎口（親指と人差し指の間）を開き、左肘をはさむように添える。

【足の動作】
左足はそのままにして、右足を前に交差する。

【留意点】顔はそのまま。

【手の動作】
左前腕左側面下段受け（甲下向き）。右掌は左肘に添えたまま。

【足の動作】
左足を東へすり出し騎馬立ち。

【手の動作】
左拳を開掌し左腰に引くとともに、右拳（甲前向き）を左掌につけて構え。

【足の動作】
立ち方はそのまま。

【留意点】
顔は西を向く。

【Hands】
Execute a Chudan-Uke to the left side with the left forearm. The right forearm is held horizontally in front of the chest (Kou is up).

【Feet】
Strongly step the left foot to the east into a Kibadachi.

【Hands】
Execute a Gedan-Uke in front with the left forearm (Kou is down). With the right hand, open the Ko-kou (thumb and fingers in the shape of a tiger's mouth) and place the left elbow on the Ko-kou as if biting it.

【Feet】
Keeping the left leg in place, cross the right foot in front of the left foot.

【Note】
The face is still keeping east.

【Hands】
Execute a Gedan-Uke to the left side with the left forearm (Kou is down). The right palm remains attached to the left elbow.

【Feet】
Slide the left foot out to the east into a Kibadachi.

【Hands】
The left hand is open and pulled to the left hip, and the right fist (Kou is forward) is positioned with the left palm.

【Feet】
Same as in ⑮.

【Note】
Turn the face to the west.

挙動 10	挙動 11-1	挙動 11-2	途中
⑰	⑱	⑲	⑳

横　　横

【手の動作】
右前腕右側面中段受け（甲下向き）。左掌右手首に添える。

【足の動作】
立ち方はそのまま。

【手の動作】
左掌は右拳前につけ（左掌甲前向き）、右拳は右腰に引く（右拳甲下向き）。

【足の動作】
右膝を右胸前にかい込む。

【留意点】
顔は南を向く。右膝、両手の動きは同時。

【手の動作】
右前猿臂（右拳甲上向き）。左掌水月前に立てる（甲後ろ向き）。

【足の動作】
右足を西へ強く踏み込み、騎馬立ち。

【手の動作】
右掌は虎口を開き縦に弧を描く。左拳左腰に引く。

【足の動作】
立ち方はそのまま。

【留意点】
顔は西を向く。肘はやや曲げてゆっくり力を込める。

【Hands】
Execute a Chudan-Uke to the right side with right forearm (Kou is down). Place the left palm on the right wrist.

【Feet】
Same as in ⑮.

【Hands】
Place the left palm in front of the right fist (left palm kou is forward) and pull the right fist toward the right hip (right fist kou is down).

【Feet】
Pull the right knee up in front of the right chest.

【Note】
Turn the face to the south. Both hands should move simultaneously with the right knee.

【Hands】
Execute a Enpi (elbow strike) in front of the right (Kou of right fist is up). Left palm standing up in front of the solar plexus (Kou is back)

【Feet】
Strongly step the right foot to the west into a Kibadachi.

【Hands】
The right palm opens in Ko-kou position and draws and upwards flowing vertical arc. Pull the left fist towards the left hip.

【Feet】
Same as in ⑲.

【Note】
Turn the face to the west. Bend the elbows slightly. Apply strength slowly.

挙動12	挙動13	挙動14	途中

㉑	㉒	㉓	㉔

【手の動作】
右掌右側面中段つかみ受け。左拳左腰。

【足の動作】
立ち方はそのまま。

【手の動作】
左拳鉤突き。右拳右腰に引く。

【足の動作】
立ち方はそのまま。

【手の動作】
両手はそのまま。

【足の動作】
右足はそのままにして、左足を前に交差する。

【留意点】
ゆっくり足を運ぶ。

【手の動作】
両手はそのまま。

【足の動作】
右膝を右胸前にかい込む。

【留意点】
顔は南を向く。

【Hands】
Execute a Chudan-Tsukami-Uke to the right side with the right palm. Left fist on the left hip.

【Feet】
Same as in ⓲.

【Hands】
Execute a Left-Kagi-Zuki. Pull the right fist back to the right hip.

【Feet】
Same as in ⓲.

【Hands】
Same as in ㉒.

【Feet】
Keeping the right foot in the same position, cross the left foot in front.

【Note】
Do slowly.

【Hands】
Same as in ㉒.

【Feet】
Pull the right knee up in front of the right chest.

【Note】
Turn the face to the south.

挙動 15	挙動 16-1	挙動 16-2	挙動 17

【手の動作】
左中段外受け。右拳はそのまま。

【足の動作】
右足を西へ強く踏み込み、騎馬立ち。

【手の動作】
右背腕上段流し受け（甲右向き）。左下段受け。

【足の動作】
立ち方はそのまま。

【手の動作】
右拳上段裏突き。左前腕胸前水平構え。

【足の動作】
立ち方はそのまま。

【留意点】
気合い

【手の動作】
右拳を開掌し右腰に引くとともに、左拳（甲前向き）を右掌につけて構える。

【足の動作】
立ち方はそのまま。

【留意点】
顔は東を向く。

【Hands】
Execute a Left-Chudan-Soto-Uke. Keep the right fist is place.

【Feet】
Strongly stamp right foot toward west into a Kibadachi.

【Hands】
Execute a Jodan-Nagashi-Uke with the outside of the right arm (Kou is out side), and a Left-Gedan-Uke (Kou is upward).

【Feet】
Same as in ㉕.

【Hands】
Execute a Right-Jodan-Ura-Zuki bring the left fist to under the right elbow.

【Feet】
Same as in ㉕.

【Note】
Kiai.

【Hands】
The right hand is open and pulled to the right hip, and the left fist (Kou is forward) is positioned with the right palm.

【Feet】
Same as in ㉕.

【Note】
Turn the face to the east.

挙動 18	挙動 19-1	挙動 19-2	途中

【手の動作】
左前腕左側面中段受け（甲下向き）。右掌左手首に添える。

【足の動作】
立ち方はそのまま。

【手の動作】
右掌は左拳前につけ（右掌甲前向き）、左拳は左腰に引く（左拳甲下向き）。

【足の動作】
左膝を左胸前にかい込む。

【留意点】
顔は南を向く。左膝、両手の動きは同時。

【手の動作】
左前猿臂（左拳甲上向き）。右掌水月前に立てる（甲後ろ向き）。

【足の動作】
左足を東へ強く踏み込み、騎馬立ち。

【手の動作】
左掌は虎口を開き縦に弧を描く。右拳右腰に引く。

【足の動作】
立ち方はそのまま。

【留意点】
顔は東を向く。肘はやや曲げてゆっくり力を込める。

【Hands】
Execute a Chudan-Uke to the left side with left forearm (Kou is down). Place the right palm on the left wrist.

【Feet】
Same as in ㉕.

【Hands】
Place the right palm in front of the left fist (right palm kou is forward) and pull the left fist toward the left hip (left fist kou is down).

【Feet】
Pull the left knee up in front of the left chest.

【Note】
Turn the face to the south.
Both hands should move simultaneously with the right knee.

【Hands】
Execute a Enpi (elbow strike) in front of the left (Kou of left fist is up). Right palm standing up in front of the solar plexus (Kou is back)

【Feet】
Strongly step the left foot to the east into a Kibadachi.

【Hands】
The left palm opens in Ko-kou position and draws and upwards flowing vertical arc. Pull the right fist towards the right hip.

【Feet】
Same as in ㉛.

【Note】
Turn the face to the east. Bend the elbows slightly. Apply strength slowly.

挙動20	挙動21	挙動22	途中

③③	③④	③⑤	③⑥

【手の動作】
左掌左側面中段つかみ受け。右拳右腰。

【足の動作】
立ち方はそのまま。

【手の動作】
右拳鉤突き。左拳左腰に引く。

【足の動作】
立ち方はそのまま。

【手の動作】
両手はそのまま。

【足の動作】
左足はそのままにして、右足を前に交差する。

【留意点】
ゆっくり足を運ぶ。

【手の動作】
両手はそのまま。

【足の動作】
左膝を左胸前にかい込む。

【留意点】
顔は南を向く。

【Hands】
Execute a Chudan-Tsukami-Uke to the left side with the left palm. Right fist on the right hip.

【Feet】
Same as in ③①.

【Hands】
Execute a Right-Kagi-Zuki. Pull the left fist back to the left hip.

【Feet】
Same as in ③①.

【Hands】
Same as in ③④.

【Feet】
Keeping the left foot in the same position, cross the right foot in front.

【Note】
Do slowly.

【Hands】
Same as in ③④.

【Feet】
Pull the left knee up in front of the left chest.

【Note】
Turn the face to the south.

挙動 23	挙動 24-1	挙動 24-2	止め

㊲	㊳	㊴	㊵

【手の動作】
右中段外受け。左拳はそのまま。

【足の動作】
左足を東へ強く踏み込み、騎馬立ち。

【手の動作】
左背腕上段流し受け（甲左向き）。右下段受け。

【足の動作】
立ち方はそのまま。

【手の動作】
左拳上段裏突き。右前腕胸前水平構え。

【足の動作】
立ち方はそのまま。

【留意点】
気合い

【手の動作】
両拳を大腿前にもっていく。

【足の動作】
右足を引き、八字立ち。

【Hands】
Execute a Right-Chudan-Soto-Uke. Keep the left fist is place.

【Feet】
Strongly stamp left foot toward the east into a Kibadachi.

【Hands】
Execute a Jodan-Nagashi-Uke with the outside of the left arm (Kou is out side), and a Right-Gedan-Uke (Kou is upward).

【Feet】
Same as in ㊲.

【Hands】
Execute a Left-Jodan-Ura-Zuki bring the right fist to under the left elbow.

【Feet】
Same as in ㊲.

【Note】
Kiai.

【Hands】
Place both fists in front of the thighs.

【Feet】
Pull the right foot harf a step into a Hachijidachi.

直立	礼	直立
 ㊶	 ㊷	 ㊸

【手の動作】
両手は開いて大腿部両側に付けて伸ばす。

【足の動作】
左足、右足の順に閉じ、結び立ち。

礼をする。

【手の動作】
手はそのまま。

【足の動作】
足はそのまま。

【Hands】
Open both hands and extend them down along the sides of the thighs.

【Feet】
Musubidachi.

∗ Bow (Rei).

【Hands】
Same as in ㊶.

【Feet】
Same as in ㊶.

鉄騎二段

鉄騎三段
Tekki Sandan
（36 挙動）

糸洲安恒先生が鉄騎初段・二段の技法を集約させて完成した形であり、体育上の鍛練形として創作されたといわれている。鉄騎二段と同じ横一文字の演武線である。この形では正確な騎馬立ちのもとで中段の受け替えなどに素早い呼吸と動きを体得しなければない。

This kata is said to have been created by Anko Itosu sensei as a kata for physical training by integrating the techniques of Tekki Shodan and Tekki Nidan. Like Tekki Nidan, it is performed with a single horizontal line. In this kata, one must master quick breathing and movements for changing Chudan guards under precise Kibadachi.

鉄騎三段　挙動一覧

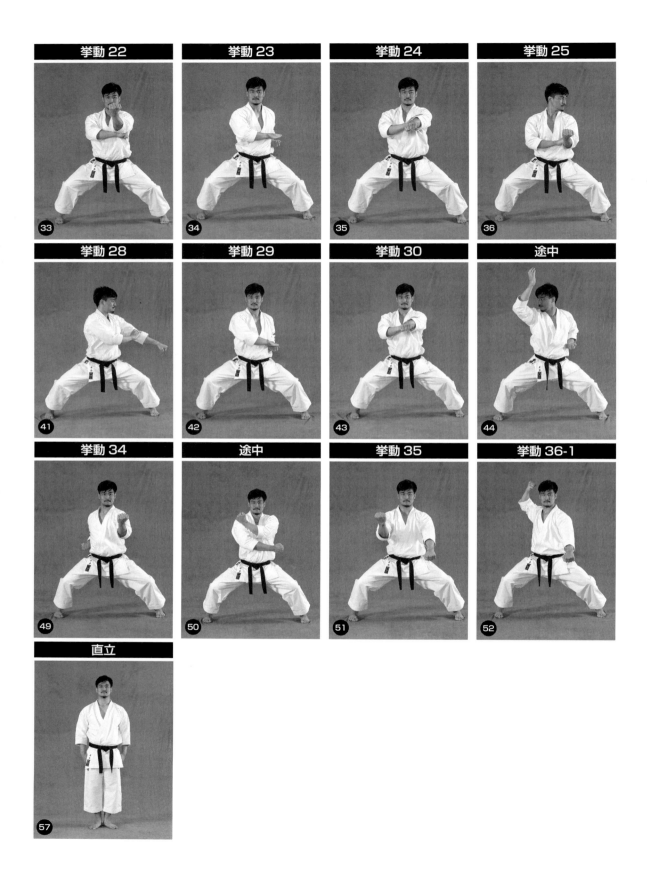

鉄騎三段　各拳動解説

直立	礼	直立	用意

①	②	③	④

【手の動作】
両手は開いて大腿部両側につけて伸ばす。

【足の動作】
結び立ち（左右とも正面に対して約30度）。

礼をする。

【手の動作】
手はそのまま。

【足の動作】
立ち方はそのまま。

【手の動作】
両拳を大腿部前にもっていく。

【足の動作】
左足、右足の順に開いて八字立ち。

【Hands】
Open both hands and extend them down along the sides of the thighs.

【Feet】
Musubidachi (left and right feet are angled approximately 30 degrees from the front).

* Bow (Rei).

【Hands】
Same as in ①.

【Feet】
Same as in ①.

【Hands】
Place both fists in front of the thighs.

【Feet】
From a Musubidachi, move the left foot, then right foot, out into a Hachijidachi.

* Explanation of terms in the text.
　Kou : The back of the hand
　Hira : The palm of the hand

挙動1	途中	挙動2	挙動3

❺	❻	❼	❽

【手の動作】
左中段外受け。右拳右腰に引く。

【足の動作】
右足を西へすり出し騎馬立ち。

【手の動作】
左腕を上にして両拳を胸前で交差する。

【足の動作】
立ち方はそのまま。

【手の動作】
右中段外受け。左下段受け。

【足の動作】
立ち方はそのまま。

【手の動作】
右前腕中段払い（甲前向き）。左前腕胸前水平構え（甲上）。

【足の動作】
立ち方はそのまま。

【留意点】
右前腕を左に打ち込むように払う。

【Hands】
Execute a Left-Chudan-Soto-Uke. Pull the right fist back to the right hip.

【Feet】
Slide the right foot out to the west into a Kibadachi.

【Hands】
Right arm in front of the belly, left arm above it, left fist in front of the right tip of shoulder (Kou is forward).

【Feet】
Same as in ❺.

【Hands】
Execute a Right-Chudan-Soto-Uke and Left-Gedan-Uke.

【Feet】
Same as in ❺.

【Hands】
Execute a Chudan-Barai with the right forearm (Kou is forward). The left forearm in horizontal position in front of the chest (Kou is upward).

【Feet】
Same as in ❺.

【Note】
Sweep the right forearm in a striking manner to the left side.

挙動4	挙動5	挙動6	挙動7
 ⑨	 ⑩	 ⑪	 ⑫

拡大

【手の動作】
右背腕上段流し受け（甲右向き）。左手はそのまま。

【足の動作】
立ち方はそのまま。

【手の動作】
右拳上段裏突き（右肘は左拳の上）。左手はそのまま。

【足の動作】
立ち方はそのまま。

【留意点】
挙動3〜5は連続する。

【手の動作】
右拳を右腰に引く（甲下向き）。左掌右拳上（甲上向き）。

【足の動作】
立ち方はそのまま。

【留意点】
左拳は四指を揃えて伸ばす。

【手の動作】
右拳中段突き（甲上向き）。左掌は虎口にして右腕をはさむ。

【足の動作】
立ち方はそのまま。

【留意点】
挙動6〜7は連続する。

【Hands】
Execute a Jodan-Nagashi-Uke with the outside of the right arm (Kou is outward). Keep the left fist is place.

【Feet】
Same as in ❺.

【Hands】
Execute a Right-Jodan-Ura-Zuki bring the left fist to under the right elbow. Keep the left fist is place.

【Feet】
Same as in ❺.

【Note】
❽ to ❿ are continuous.

【Hands】
Pull the right fist toward the right hip (Kou is down). Place left palm on top of right fist (Kou is up).

【Feet】
Same as in ❺.

【Note】
Extend and keep the left hand's four fingers together side by side.

【Hands】
Execute a Right-Chudan-Zuki(Kou is up). Make Ko-kou with the left palm and grasp the inside of the right elbow.

【Feet】
Same as in ❺.

【Note】
⓫ and ⓬ are continuous.

挙動8	挙動9	挙動10	途中
⑬	 ⑭	 ⑮	 ⑯

【手の動作】
右前腕をひねりながら右肘を軽く引く。左掌は右肘に添えたまま。

【足の動作】
立ち方はそのまま。

【留意点】
顔は西を向く。

【手の動作】
両手はそのまま。

【足の動作】
右足はそのままにして、左足を前に交差する。

【留意点】
ゆっくり足を運ぶ。

【手の動作】
右前腕右側面下段受け（甲下向き）。左掌は右肘に添えたまま。

【足の動作】
右足を西へすり出し騎馬立ち。

【手の動作】
左掌は右肘に添えたまま。右拳を返しながら、右肩を中心に大きく弧を描く。

【足の動作】
立ち方はそのまま。

【Hands】
While twisting the right forearm, relax and slightly pull the right elbow, (Kou is down). Keep the left palm positioned on the right inner elbow.

【Feet】
Same as in ❺.

【Note】
Turn the face to the west.

【Hands】
Same as in ⑬.

【Feet】
Keeping the right leg in place, cross the left foot in front of the right foot.

【Note】
Do slowly.

【Hands】
Execute a Gedan-Uke to the right side with the right forearm (Kou is down). The left palm remains attached to the right elbow.

【Feet】
Slide the right foot out to the west into a Kibadachi.

【Hands】
Keep the left palm on the right inner elbow. While pulling the right fist, draw a large arc around the right shoulder.

【Feet】
Same as in ⑮.

【手の動作】
右拳右側面下段振り捨て（甲上向き）。左掌は右肘に添えたまま。

【足の動作】
立ち方はそのまま。

【手の動作】
右拳を右腰に引く（甲下向き）。左掌右拳上（甲上向き）。

【足の動作】
立ち方はそのまま。

【留意点】
顔は南を向く。

【手の動作】
右拳中段突き（甲上向き）。左掌は虎口にして右腕をはさむ。

【足の動作】
立ち方はそのまま。

【留意点】
挙動12〜13は連続する。

【Hands】
Execute a Gedan-Furisute to the right side with the right fist (Kou is up). Hold the left palm on the inner right elbow.

【Feet】
Same as in ⓯.

【Hands】
Pull the right fist toward the right hip (Kou is down). Place left palm on top of the right fist (Kou is up).

【Feet】
Same as in ⓯.

【Note】
Turn the face to the south.

【Hands】
Execute a Right-Chudan-Zuki (Kou is up). Make Ko-kou with the left palm and grasp the inside of the right elbow.

【Feet】
Same as in ⓯.

【Note】
⓳ and ⓴ are continuous.

【手の動作】
左腕を上にして両拳を胸前で交差する。

【足の動作】
立ち方はそのまま。

【手の動作】
右中段外受け。左下段受け。

【足の動作】
立ち方はそのまま。

【手の動作】
右腕を上にして両拳を胸前で交差する。

【足の動作】
立ち方はそのまま。

【手の動作】
左中段外受け。右下段受け。

【足の動作】
立ち方はそのまま。

【Hands】
Right arm in front of the belly, left arm above it, left fist in front of the right tip of shoulder (Kou is forward).

【Feet】
Same as in ⓯.

【Hands】
Execute a Right-Chudan-Soto-Uke and Left- Gedan-Uke.

【Feet】
Same as in ⓯.

【Hands】
Left arm in front of the belly, right arm above it, right fist in front of the left tip of shoulder (Kou is forward).

【Feet】
Same as in ⓯.

【Hands】
Execute a Left-Chudan-Soto-Uke and Right- Gedan-Uke.

【Feet】
Same as in ⓯.

挙動 16-1	挙動 16-2	挙動 17	挙動 18

㉕	㉖	㉗	㉘

【手の動作】
左背腕上段流し受け（甲左向き）。右手はそのまま。

【足の動作】
立ち方はそのまま。

【手の動作】
左拳上段裏突き。右前腕胸前水平構え。

【足の動作】
立ち方はそのまま。

【留意点】
挙動15〜16は連続する。
気合い。

【手の動作】
両手はそのまま。

【足の動作】
立ち方はそのまま。

【留意点】
顔は東を向く。

【手の動作】
両手はそのまま。

【足の動作】
左足はそのままにして、右足を前に交差する。

【留意点】
ゆっくり足を運ぶ。

【Hands】
Execute a Jodan-Nagashi-Uke with the outside of the left arm (Kou is out side). Keep the right fist is place.

【Feet】
Same as in ⑮.

【Hands】
Execute a Left-Jodan-Ura-Zuki bring the right fist to under the left elbow.

【Feet】
Same as in ⑮.

【Note】
㉔ to ㉖ are continuous.
Kiai.

【Hands】
Same as in ㉖.

【Feet】
Same as in ⑮.

【Note】
Turn the face to the east.

【Hands】
Same as in ㉖.

【Feet】
Keeping the left foot in the same position, cross the right foot in front.

【Note】
Do slowly.

途中	挙動 19	挙動 20	挙動 21

㉙　㉚　㉛　㉜

【手の動作】
両手はそのまま。

【足の動作】
左膝を左胸前にかい込む。

【手の動作】
両手はそのまま。

【足の動作】
左足を東へ強く踏み込み、騎馬立ち。

【留意点】
左足を踏み込むと同時に、顔を南へ向ける。

【手の動作】
左前腕中段払い（甲前向き）。右手はそのまま。

【足の動作】
立ち方はそのまま。

【留意点】
左前腕を右へ打ち込むように払う。

【手の動作】
左背腕上段流し受け（甲左向き）。右手はそのまま。

【足の動作】
立ち方はそのまま。

【Hands】
Same as in ㉖.

【Feet】
Bring up left knee to in front of left side of chest.

【Hands】
Same as in ㉖.

【Feet】
Strongly stamp left foot toward the east into a Kibadachi.

【Note】
Step into the left foot and turn the face to the south simultaneously.

【Hands】
Execute a Chudan-Barai with the left forearm (Kou is forward). Keep the right fist is place.

【Feet】
Same as in ㉚.

【Note】
Sweep the left forearm in a striking manner to the right side.

【Hands】
Execute a Jodan-Nagashi-Uke with the outside of the left arm (Kou is outward). Keep the right fist is place.

【Feet】
Same as in ㉚.

挙動 22	挙動 23	挙動 24	挙動 25

㉝	㉞	㉟	㊱

【手の動作】
左拳上段裏突き（左肘は右拳の上）。右手はそのまま。

【足の動作】
立ち方はそのまま。

【留意点】
挙動 20 ～ 22 は連続する。

【手の動作】
左拳を左腰に引く（甲下向き）。右掌左拳上（甲上向き）。

【足の動作】
立ち方はそのまま。

【留意点】
右拳は四指を揃えて伸ばす。

【手の動作】
左拳中段突き。（甲上向き）。右掌は虎口にして左腕をはさむ。

【足の動作】
立ち方はそのまま。

【留意点】
挙動 23 ～ 24 は続ける。

【手の動作】
左前腕をひねりながら左肘を軽く引く。右掌は左肘に添えたまま。

【足の動作】
立ち方はそのまま。

【留意点】
顔は東を向く。

【Hands】
Execute a Left-Jodan-Ura-Zuki bring the right fist to under the left elbow. Keep the right fist is place.

【Feet】
Same as in ㉚.

【Note】
㉛ to ㉝ are continuous.

【Hands】
Pull the left fist toward the left hip (Kou is down). Place right palm on top of left fist (Kou is up).

【Feet】
Same as in ㉚.

【Note】
Extend and keep the right hand's four fingers together side by side.

【Hands】
Execute a Left-Chudan-Zuki(Kou is up). Make Ko-kou with the right palm and grasp the inside of the left elbow.

【Feet】
Same as in ㉚.

【Note】
㉞ and ㉟ are continuous.

【Hands】
While twisting the left forearm, relax and slightly pull the left elbow, (Kou is down). Keep the right palm positioned on the left inner elbow.

【Feet】
Same as in ㉚.

【Note】
Turn the face to the east.

挙動 26

挙動 27

途中

途中

【手の動作】
両手はそのまま。

【足の動作】
左足はそのままにして、右足を前に交差する。

【留意点】
ゆっくり足を運ぶ。

【手の動作】
左前腕左側面下段受け（甲下向き）。右掌は左肘に添えたまま。

【足の動作】
左足を東へすり出し騎馬立ち。

【手の動作】
右掌を左肘に添えたまま。左拳を返しながら、左肩を中心に大きく弧を縦に描く。

【足の動作】
立ち方はそのまま。

【Hands】
Same as in 36 .

【Feet】
Keeping the left leg in place, cross the right foot in front of the left foot.

【Note】
Do slowly.

【Hands】
Execute a Gedan-Uke to the left side with the left forearm (Kou is down). The right palm remains attached to the left elbow.

【Feet】
Slide the left foot out to the east and stand in Kibadachi.

【Hands】
Keep the right palm on the left inner elbow. While pulling the left fist, draw a large arc around the left shoulder.

【Feet】
Same as in 38 .

挙動 28	挙動 29	挙動 30	途中

㊶	㊷	㊸	㊹

【手の動作】
左拳左側面下段振り捨て（甲上向き）。右掌は左肘に添えたまま。

【足の動作】
立ち方はそのまま。

【手の動作】
左拳を左腰に引く（甲下向き）。右掌左拳上（甲上向き）。

【足の動作】
立ち方はそのまま。

【留意点】
顔は南を向く。

【手の動作】
左拳中段突き（甲上向き）。右掌は虎口にして左腕をはさむ。

【足の動作】
立ち方はそのまま。

【留意点】
挙動29～30は続ける。

【手の動作】
右掌は縦に弧を描く（甲上向き）。左拳左腰に引く。

【足の動作】
立ち方はそのまま。

【留意点】
顔は西を向く。肘はやや曲げてゆっくり力を込める。

【Hands】
Execute a Gedan-Furisute to the left side with the left fist (Kou is up). Hold the right palm on the inner left elbow.

【Feet】
Same as in ㊳.

【Hands】
Pull the left fist toward the left hip (Kou is down). Place right palm on top of left fist (Kou is up).

【Feet】
Same as in ㊳.

【Note】
Turn the face to the south.

【Hands】
Execute a Left-Chudan-Zuki(Kou is up). Make Ko-kou with the right palm and grasp the inside of the left elbow.

【Feet】
Same as in ㊳.

【Note】
㊷ and ㊸ are continuous.

【Hands】
The right palm opens in Ko-kou position and draws and upwards flowing vertical arc. Pull the left fist towards the left hip.

【Feet】
Same as in ㊳.

【Note】
Turn the face to the west. Bend the elbows slightly. Apply strength slowly.

挙動31	挙動32	挙動33	途中

㊺	㊻	㊼	㊽

【手の動作】
右掌右側面中段つかみ受け。左拳左腰。

【足の動作】
立ち方はそのまま。

【手の動作】
左拳鉤突き。右拳右腰に引く。

【足の動作】
立ち方はそのまま。

【手の動作】
両手はそのまま。

【足の動作】
右足はそのままにして、左足を前に交差する。

【留意点】
ゆっくり足を運ぶ。

【手の動作】
両手はそのまま。

【足の動作】
右膝を右胸前にかい込む。

【留意点】
顔は南を向く。

【Hands】
Execute a Chudan-Tsukami-Uke to the right side with the right palm. Left fist on left hip.

【Feet】
Same as in ㊳.

【Hands】
Execute a Left-Kagi-Zuki. Pull the right fist back to the right hip.

【Feet】
Same as in ㊳.

【Hands】
Same as in ㊻.

【Feet】
Keeping right foot in the same position, cross left foot in front.

【Note】
Do slowly.

【Hands】
Same as in ㊻.

【Feet】
Pull the right knee up in front of the right chest.

【Note】
Turn the face to the south.

挙動 34	途中	挙動 35	挙動 36-1

㊾	㊿	㊿①	㊿②

【手の動作】
左中段外受け。右拳はそのまま。

【足の動作】
右足を西へ強く踏み込み、騎馬立ち。

【手の動作】
左腕を上にして両拳を胸前で交差する。

【足の動作】
立ち方はそのまま。

【手の動作】
右中段外受け。左下段受け。

【足の動作】
立ち方はそのまま。

【手の動作】
右背腕上段流し受け（甲右向き）。左手はそのまま。

【足の動作】
立ち方はそのまま。

【Hands】
Execute a Left-Chudan-Soto-Uke. Keep the right fist is place.

【Feet】
Strongly stamp right foot toward west into a Kibadachi.

【Hands】
Right arm in front of the belly, left arm above it, left fist in front of the right tip of shoulder (Kou is forward).

【Feet】
Same as in ㊾.

【Hands】
Execute a Right-Chudan-Soto-Uke and Left-Gedan-Uke.

【Feet】
Same as in ㊾.

【Hands】
Execute a Jodan-Nagashi-Uke with the outside of the right arm (Kou is outward). Keep the left fist is place.

【Feet】
Same as in ㊾.

挙動36-2	止め	直立	礼

【手の動作】
右拳上段裏突き。左前腕胸前水平構え。

【足の動作】
立ち方はそのまま。

【留意点】
挙動35～36は続ける。
気合い。

【手の動作】
両拳を大腿部前にもっていく。

【足の動作】
右足を引き、八字立ち。

【手の動作】
両手は開いて大腿部両側に付けて伸ばす。

【足の動作】
左足、右足の順に閉じ、結び立ち。

礼をする。

【Hands】
Execute a Right-Jodan-Ura-Zuki bring the left fist to under the right elbow.

【Feet】
Same as in ㊾.

【Note】
㉛ to ㊳ are continuous.
Kiai.

【Hands】
Place both fists in front of the thighs.

【Feet】
Pull the right foot harf a step into a Hachijidachi.

【Hands】
Open both hands and extend them down along the sides of the thighs.

【Feet】
Musubidachi.

＊ Bow (Rei).

直立

【手の動作】
手はそのまま。

【足の動作】
足はそのまま。

【Hands】
Same as in 55.

【Feet】
Same as in 55.

鉄騎二段

半月
Hangetsu
(41 挙動)

　この形は足の運び方が半月を描くことから、この名が付けられたとされている。呼吸に合せて手足同時に動く動作、半月形の足のすり出しなどが特徴である。後半では上体を動かさないで、素早く後足を前足に交差させ、間合いを接近して攻め込む技術が含まれている。半月立ちは前屈立ちと三戦立ちの中間の立ち方であり、三戦立ちから前足を一足長半前に出して立つ。

　This kata is said to be so named because of the way its feet move in a Hangetsu (half-moon) pattern. It is characterized by movements in which the arms and legs move simultaneously with the breath, and the movement of the foot sliding out in a half-moon shape. The second half includes the technique of quickly crossing the rear foot over the front foot without moving the upper body and attacking close to enemy. Hangetsudachi is an intermediate standing style between Zenkutsudachi and Sanchindachi, in which the front foot is brought forward one and a half feet from the Sanchindachi.

半月　挙動一覧

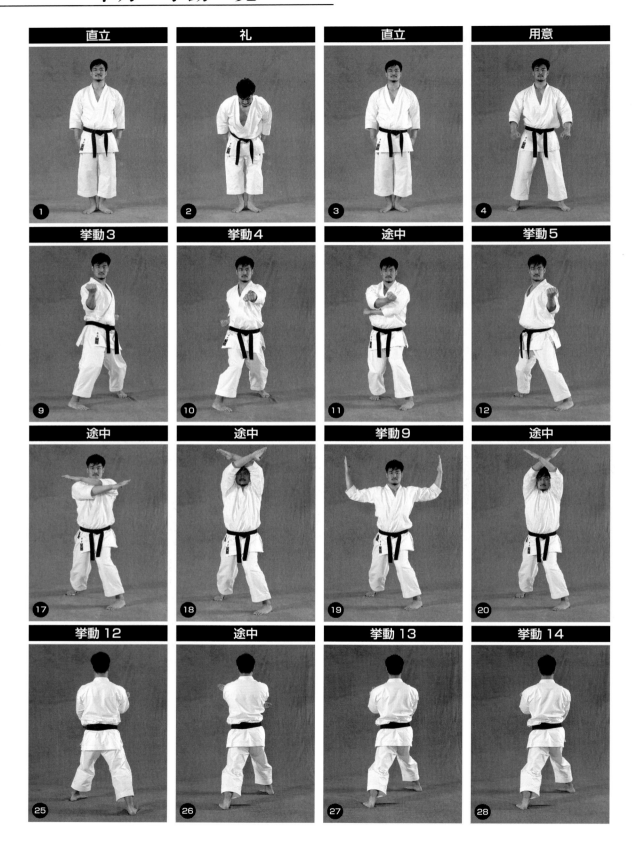

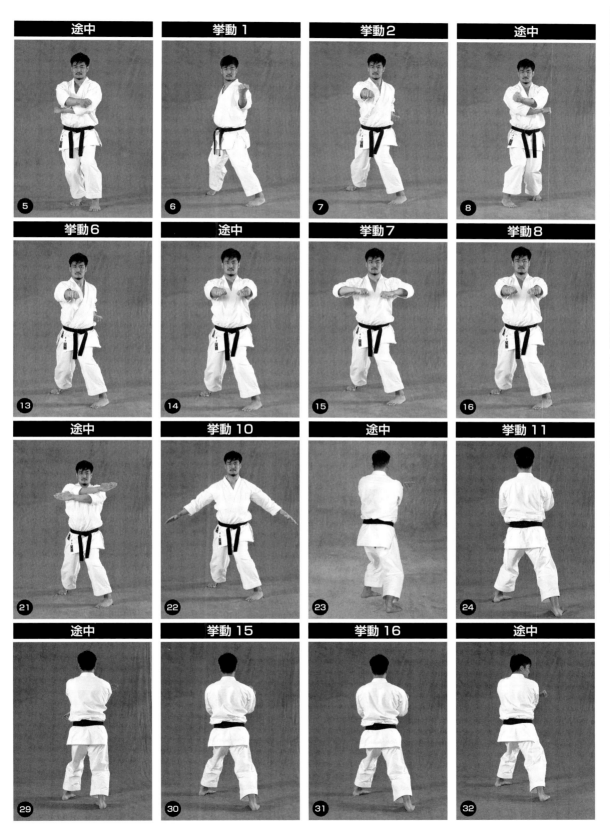

半月　各挙動解説

直立	礼	直立	用意

❶	❷	❸	❹

【手の動作】
両手は開いて大腿部両側につけて伸ばす。

【足の動作】
結び立ち（左右とも正面に対して約30度）。

礼をする。

【手の動作】
手はそのまま。

【足の動作】
立ち方はそのまま。

【手の動作】
両拳を大腿部前にもっていく。

【足の動作】
左足、右足の順に開いて八字立ち。

【Hands】
Open both hands and extend them down along the sides of the thighs.

【Feet】
Musubidachi (left and right feet are angled approximately 30 degrees from the front).

* Bow (Rei).

【Hands】
Same as in ❶.

【Feet】
Same as in ❶.

【Hands】
Place both fists in front of the thighs.

【Feet】
From a Musubidachi, move the left foot, then right foot, out into a Hachijidachi.

* Explanation of terms in the text.
   Kou : The back of the hand
   Hira : The palm of the hand

途中	挙動1	挙動2	途中
⑤	⑥	⑦	⑧

【手の動作】
右拳を前に出し、左拳を右脇腹にもっていく。

【足の動作】
左足を内側から弧を描いて南へすり出す。

【留意点】
ゆっくり。

【手の動作】
左中段外受け。右拳右腰に引く。

【足の動作】
左足前半月立ち。

【留意点】
手足同時にゆっくりきめ、呼吸と動作を合わせる。
半月立ちは三戦立ちの前足を一足長前に置く。

【手の動作】
右中段逆突き。左拳左腰に引く。

【足の動作】
立ち方はそのまま。

【留意点】
腰の回転と両手の動きを呼吸にゆっくり合わせる。

【手の動作】
左拳を前に出し、右拳を左脇腹にもっていく。

【足の動作】
右足を内側から弧を描いて南へすり出す。

【留意点】
ゆっくり。

【Hands】
Extend the right fist forward, bring the left fist to the right side of the body.

【Feet】
Draw an arc from the inside with the left foot and move to the south.

【Note】
Do slowly.

【Hands】
Execute a Left-Chudan-Soto-Uke. Pull the right fist back to the right hip.

【Feet】
Left-Hangetsudachi.

【Note】
Slowly move the arms and legs simultaneously, coordinating the breathing with the movements. Hangestsudachi is similar to Sanchindachi, with the exception that the front foot is launched forward by one foot-size towards the front.

【Hands】
Execute a Right-Chudan-Gyaku-Zuki. Pull the left fist back to the left hip.

【Feet】
Same as in ⑥.

【Note】
Slowly synchronize the rotation of the hips and the movement of the hands with the breathing.

【Hands】
Extend the left fist forward, bring the right fist to the left side of the body.

【Feet】
Draw an arc from the inside with the right foot and move to the south.

【Note】
Do slowly.

挙動3	挙動4	途中	挙動5

❾	❿	⓫	⓬

【手の動作】
右中段外受け。左拳左腰に引く。

【足の動作】
右足前半月立ち。

【留意点】
ゆっくり。

【手の動作】
左中段逆突き。右拳右腰に引く。

【足の動作】
立ち方はそのまま。

【留意点】
ゆっくり。

【手の動作】
右拳を前に出し、左拳を右脇腹にもっていく。

【足の動作】
左足を内側から弧を描いて南へすり出す。

【留意点】
ゆっくり。

【手の動作】
左中段外受け。右拳右腰に引く。

【足の動作】
左足前半月立ち。

【留意点】
ゆっくり。

【Hands】
Execute a Right-Chudan-Soto-Uke. Pull the left fist back to the left hip.

【Feet】
Right-Hangetsudachi.

【Note】
Do slowly.

【Hands】
Execute a Left-Chudan-Gyaku-Zuki. Pull the right fist back to the right hip.

【Feet】
Same as in ❾.

【Note】
Do slowly.

【Hands】
Extend the right fist forward, bring the left fist to the right side of the body.

【Feet】
Draw an arc from the inside with the left foot and move to the south.

【Note】
Do slowly.

【Hands】
Execute a Left-Chudan-Soto-Uke. Pull the right fist back to the right hip.

【Feet】
Left-Hangetsudachi.

【Note】
Do slowly.

挙動6	途中	挙動7	挙動8
⑬	⑭	⑮	⑯

【手の動作】
右中段逆突き。左拳左腰に引く。

【足の動作】
立ち方はそのまま。

【留意点】
ゆっくり。

【手の動作】
右拳は示指一本拳をつくりながら肘を横に張り少し引き寄せ、左拳も示指一本拳をつくりながら少し前に突き出し、途中で左右両拳を合わせて両乳の下に引き寄せる。

【足の動作】
立ち方はそのまま。

【留意点】
ゆっくり。

【手の動作】
両示指一本拳両乳下構え（両甲上向き）。

【足の動作】
立ち方はそのまま。

【留意点】
ゆっくり。

【手の動作】
両示指一本拳中段諸手突き。

【足の動作】
立ち方はそのまま。

【留意点】
ゆっくり。

【Hands】
Execute a Right-Chudan-Gyaku-Zuki. Pull the left fist back to the left hip.

【Feet】
Same as in ⑫.

【Note】
Do slowly.

【Hands】
The right fist is held in a Jishi-Ipponken (index finger middle knuckle thrust out) while the elbow is pulled out to the side and the fist is drawn in slightly, and the left fist is also held in a Jishi-Ipponken while thrusting forward slightly, then both fists move together to draw them in front of each chest.

【Feet】
Same as in ⑫.

【Note】
Do slowly.

【Hands】
Both Jishi-Ipponken are positioned in front of each chest (Both Kou are upward).

【Feet】
Same as in ⑫.

【Note】
Do slowly.

【Hands】
Execute a Chudan-Morote-Zuki in both Jishi-Ipponken.

【Feet】
Same as in ⑫.

【Note】
Do slowly.

示指一本拳　Jishi-Ipponken

【手の動作】
両手を開掌し両手を手刀の形にして胸前で交差する。さらに交差した両手を顔の前に上げる。

【足の動作】
立ち方はそのまま。

【手の動作】
両掌山構え（両甲外向き）。

【足の動作】
立ち方はそのまま。

【留意点】
両肘は肩の高さ。ゆっくり。

【手の動作】
両手首を交差しながら肘を伸ばし下へ下げる。

【足の動作】
立ち方はそのまま。

【留意点】
ゆっくり。

【Hands】
Open the hands and make them into a Shuto shape and cross them in front of the chest. Cross hands in front of the chest then raise both hands in front of the face.

【Feet】
Same as in ⑫.

【Hands】
Make both palms (Both Kou are outside) in Yamagamae (mountain-shaped stance).

【Feet】
Same as in ⑫.

【Note】
Both elbows slowly reach shoulder height.

【Hands】
While crossing the wrists extend the elbows forward getting ready to lower them.

【Feet】
Same as in ⑫.

【Note】
Do slowly.

挙動の解釈 Application (Bunkai) of ⑰ - ㉒

【手の動作】
両掌両側下段払い。

【足の動作】
立ち方はそのまま。

【留意点】
挙動1〜10まではゆっくり極める。

【手の動作】
右掌は前腕を返して左脇腹から上へ、左掌は右肩前から下に素早く払う。

【足の動作】
左脚を軸に、右足を一歩南へすり出しながら左回転し北へ振り向く。

【手の動作】
右掌中段外受け（甲前下向き）。
左掌下段受け（甲前上向き）。

【足の動作】
左足前半月立ち。

【留意点】
気合い。

【Hands】
Execute a Gedan-barai to both sides with both palms.

【Feet】
Same as in ⓬.

【Note】
Make a Kime the movements 1 to 10 slowly.

【Hands】
Turn the right forearm and quickly sweep the right palm upwards from the left side, and the left palm downwards from in front of the right shoulder.

【Feet】
Slide one step south with the right foot and turn the body to the north with a left turn on the axis of the left foot.

【Hands】
Execute a Chudan-Soto-Uke (Kou is forward-downward) with the right palm. and a Gedan-Uke with left palm (Kou is forward-upward).

【Feet】
Left-Hangetsudachi.

【Note】
Kiai.

後ろから抱きかかえられた時、両腕を肩の横に引き上げて、相手の腕をはずす。さらに体を横に開いて下段を打つ。

When held from behind, pull the arms up to the sides of the shoulders and release the opponent's arms. Futher, open the body sideways and strike the Gedan.

挙動 12	途中	挙動 13	挙動 14

 後ろ	 後ろ	 後ろ	 後ろ

【手の動作】
右掌つかみ受け（甲上向き、虎口を開く）。左掌はそのまま。

【足の動作】
立ち方はそのまま。

【留意点】
右手首をゆっくり力入れて裏返しながら、右肘を右脇に少し引き寄せる。

【手の動作】
右掌は左肩前、左掌は右脇下。

【足の動作】
右足を内側から弧を描いて北へすり出す。

【手の動作】
左掌中段外受け。右掌下段受け。

【足の動作】
右足前半月立ち。

【手の動作】
左掌つかみ受け（甲上向き、虎口を開く）。右掌はそのまま。

【足の動作】
立ち方はそのまま。

【留意点】
左手首をゆっくり力入れて裏返しながら、左肘を左脇に少し引き寄せる。

【Hands】
Excute a Tsukami-Uke (Kou is upward, opening Kokou) with the right palm. The left palm maintains its position.

【Feet】
Same as in ㉔.

【Note】
Slowly and forcefully turn the right wrist over and pull the right elbow slightly toward the right side.

【Hands】
The right palm goes in front of the left tip of shoulder and the left palm goes under the right armpit.

【Feet】
Draw an arc from the inside with the right foot and move to the north.

【Hands】
Execute a Chudan-Soto-Uke with the left palm, and a Gedan-Uke with right palm.

【Feet】
Right-Hangetsudachi.

【Hands】
Excute a Tsukami-Uke (Kou is upward, opening Kokou) with the left palm. The right palm maintains its position.

【Feet】
Same as in ㉔.

【Note】
Slowly and forcefully turn the left wrist over and pull the left elbow slightly toward the left side.

相手の中段突きを手刀で受け、そのまま手首を返し、つかんで引き寄せる。

Gurd the opponent's Chudan-Zuki with a Shuto, then turn the wrist and grab their Tsuki hand from the wrist and pull it.

挙動の解釈 Application (Bunkai) of ㉗-㉘

途中	挙動15	挙動16	途中
 ㉙	 ㉚	 ㉛	 ㉜
後ろ	後ろ	後ろ	後ろ
【手の動作】 左掌は右肩前、右掌は左脇下。 【足の動作】 左足を内側から弧を描いて北へすり出す。	【手の動作】 右掌中段外受け。左掌下段受け。 【足の動作】 左足前半月立ち。	【手の動作】 右掌つかみ受け（甲上向き、虎口を開く）。左掌はそのまま。 【足の動作】 立ち方はそのまま。 【留意点】 右手首をゆっくり力入れて裏返しながら、右肘を右脇に少し引き寄せる。	【手の動作】 左拳を前に出し、右拳を左脇腹にもっていく。 【足の動作】 右足を半月形に東へすり出す。

【Hands】
The left palm goes in front of the right tip of shoulder and the right palm goes under the left armpit.

【Feet】
Draw an arc from the inside with the left foot and move to the north.

【Hands】
Execute a Chudan-Soto-Uke with the right palm, and a Gedan-Uke with left palm.

【Feet】
Left-Hangetsudachi.

【Hands】
Excute a Tsukami-Uke (Kou is upward, opening Kokou) with the right palm. The left palm maintains its position.

【Feet】
Same as in ㉚.

【Note】
Slowly and forcefully turn the right wrist over and pull the right elbow slightly toward the right side.

【Hands】
Extend the left fist forward, bring the right fist to the left side of the body.

【Feet】
Slide the right foot toward the east in a "Hangetsu" (half-moon) shape.

| 挙動 17 | 挙動 18 | 挙動 19 | 途中 |

後ろ

【手の動作】
右中段外受け。左拳左腰に引く。

【足の動作】
右足前半月立ち。

【留意点】
強く速く。

【手の動作】
左中段逆突き。右拳右腰に引く。

【足の動作】
立ち方はそのまま。

【手の動作】
右中段順突き。左拳左腰に引く。

【足の動作】
立ち方はそのまま。

【留意点】
挙動18〜19は連続する。

【手の動作】
右拳を前に出し、左拳を右脇腹にもっていく。

【足の動作】
右脚を軸に左に回転し、西へ寄り足ですり出す。

【Hands】
Excute a Right-Chudan-Soto-Uke. Pull the left fist back to the left hip.

【Feet】
Right-Hangetsudachi.

【Note】
Hard and fast

【Hands】
Excute a Left-Chudan-Gyaku-Zuki. Pull the right fist back to the right hip.

【Feet】
Same as in ㉝.

【Hands】
Excute a Right-Chudan-Jun-Zuki. Pull back the left fist to the left hip.

【Feet】
Same as in ㉝.

【Note】
㉞ and ㉟ are continuous.

【Hands】
Extend the right fist forward, bring the left fist to the right side of the body.

【Feet】
Rotating the body to the left, use the right leg as the axis and slide out with Yoriashi to the west.

挙動20	挙動21	挙動22	途中

後ろ			後ろ

【手の動作】
左中段外受け。右拳右腰に引く。

【足の動作】
左足前半月立ち。

【手の動作】
右中段逆突き。左拳左腰に引く。

【足の動作】
立ち方はそのまま。

【手の動作】
左中段順突き。右拳右腰に引く。

【足の動作】
立ち方はそのまま。

【留意点】
挙動21～22は連続する。

【手の動作】
左拳を前に出し、右拳を左脇腹にもっていく。

【足の動作】
左脚を軸に右足を内側から弧を描いて北へ寄り足ですり出す。

【Hands】
Excute a Left-Chudan-Soto-Uke. Pull the right fist back to the right hip.

【Feet】
Left-Hangetsudachi.

【Hands】
Excute a Right-Chudan-Gyaku-Zuki. Pull the left fist back to the left hip.

【Feet】
Same as in ㊲.

【Hands】
Excute a Left-Chudan-Jun-Zuki. Pull back right fist to the right hip.

【Feet】
Same as in ㊲.

【Note】
㊳ and ㊴ are continuous.

【Hands】
Extend the left fist forward, bring the right fist to the left side of the body.

【Feet】
The left leg is on its axis, Arcing the right leg from the inside, and slides out in a Yoriashi to the north.

挙動 23	挙動 24	挙動 25	途中
㊶	㊷	㊸	㊹
後ろ	後ろ	後ろ	

【手の動作】
右中段外受け。左拳左腰に引く。

【足の肘動作】
右足前半月立ち。

【手の動作】
左中段逆突き。右拳右腰に引く。

【足の動作】
立ち方はそのまま。

【手の動作】
右中段順突き。左拳左腰に引く。

【足の動作】
立ち方はそのまま。

【留意点】
挙動24～25は連続する。

【手の動作】
左拳は右腰前から額前上を弧を描いてゆっくり縦に回す。右拳右腰に引く。

【足の動作】
左足裏を右膝横に引きつけ、左膝をかい込む。

【留意点】
左拳、左足は揃えてゆっくり。顔は南を向く。

【Hands】
Excute a Right-Chudan-Soto-Uke. Pull the left fist back to the left hip.

【Feet】
Right-Hangetsudachi.

【Hands】
Excute a Left-Chudan-Gyaku-Zuki. Pull the right fist back to the right hip.

【Feet】
Same as in ㊶.

【Hands】
Excute a Right-Chudan-Jun-Zuki. Pull back left fist to the left hip.

【Feet】
Same as in ㊶.

【Note】
㊷ and ㊸ are continuous.

【Hands】
Slowly rotate the left fist vertically in an arc from in front of the right hip to above the forehead. Pull the right fist to the right hip.

【Feet】
Pull the sole of the left foot to the side of the right knee while tucking the knee in.

【Note】
Maintain simultaneous slow movement with the left fist and left foot. Turn the face to the south.

挙動の解釈 Application (Bunkai) of ㊹ - ㊺

相手が後足をねらって蹴込んできた時、膝を胸にかい込んでさばき、足をおろすのと同時に裏拳縦回し打ちで相手の顔面を攻撃する。

| 途中 | 挙動26 | 挙動27 | 挙動28 |

【足の動作】
ゆっくり腰を左に回転しながら、左足を弧を描いて回し、南へつま先からおろす。

【手の動作】
左裏拳縦回し打ち。右拳右腰。

【足の動作】
右後屈立ち。

【手の動作】
両手はそのまま。

【足の動作】
右足を前に交差する。

【留意点】
足を寄せるとき両手の位置を変えない。
ゆっくり足を運ぶ。

【手の動作】
左拳右肩上へ引く。右拳はそのまま。

【足の動作】
左中段前蹴り。右脚立ち。

【留意点】
左拳の引き寄せと前蹴りは同時。

【Feet】
While slowly rotating the hips to the left, rotate the left foot in an arc and bring it down to the south, landing first on the toes.

【Hands】
Excute a Left-Uraken-Tate-Mawashi-Uchi. The right fist on the right hip.

【Feet】
Right-Kokutsudachi.

【Hands】
Same as in ㊻.

【Feet】
Cross right foot in front.

【Note】
Do not change the position of the hands when sliding the right foot.
Move the right foot slowly.

【Hands】
Pull the left fist towards the right shoulder. Keep the right fist is place.

【Feet】
Excute a Left-Chudan-Mae-Geri. Stand on the right leg.

【Note】
The pulling of the left fist and the Maegeri are done simultaneously.

When the opponent targets the back leg, lift away the knee of the back leg into the chest shifting away from the attack.
Then simultaneously lower that leg while striking opponent's face with a vertical back-fist strike.

挙動 29	挙動 30	挙動 31	途中

後ろ

【手の動作】
左拳下段突き（甲上向き）。右拳はそのまま。

【足の動作】
左足を右足前におろし、左足前半月立ち。

【手の動作】
右中段逆突き。左拳左腰に引く。

【足の動作】
立ち方はそのまま。

【留意点】
腰を左に回転する。

【手の動作】
左上段揚げ受け。右拳右腰に引く。

【足の動作】
立ち方はそのまま。

【手の動作】
右拳は左腰前から額前上を弧を描いてゆっくり縦に回す。左拳左腰に引く。

【足の動作】
右足裏を左膝横に引きつけ、右膝をかい込む。

【留意点】
右拳、右足は揃えてゆっくり。顔は北を向く。

【Hands】
Execute a Gedan-Zuki with the left fist (Kou is upward). Keep the right fist is place.

【Feet】
Drop the left foot in front of the right foot, into Left-Hangetsudachi.

【Hands】
Execute a Right-Chudan-Gyaku-Zuki. Pull the left fist back to the left hip.

【Feet】
Same as in ㊾.

【Note】
Rotate the hips to the left.

【Hands】
Execute a Left-Jodan-Age-Uke. Pull the right fist back to the right hip.

【Feet】
Same as in ㊾.

【Hands】
Slowly rotate the right fist vertically in an arc from in front of the left hip to above the forehead. Pull the left fist to the left hip.

【Feet】
Pull the sole of the right foot to the side of the left knee while tucking the knee in.

【Note】
Maintain simultaneous slow movement with the right fist and right foot. Turn the face to the north.

挙動の解釈 Application (Bunkai) of ㊾ - ㊿

途中	挙動32	挙動33	挙動34

後ろ	後ろ	後ろ	後ろ

【足の動作】
ゆっくり腰を右に回転しながら、右足を弧を描いて回し、北へつま先からおろす。

【手の動作】
右裏拳縦回し打ち。左拳左腰。

【足の動作】
左後屈立ち。

【手の動作】
両手はそのまま。

【足の動作】
左足を前に交差する。

【留意点】
足を寄せるとき両手の位置を変えない。
ゆっくり。

【手の動作】
右拳左肩上へ引く。左拳はそのまま。

【足の動作】
右中段前蹴り。左脚立ち。

【留意点】
右拳の引き寄せと前蹴りは同時。

【Feet】
While slowly rotating the hips to the right, rotate the right foot in an arc and bring it down to the north, landing first on the toes.

【Hands】
Excute a Right-Uraken-Tate-Mawashi-Uchi. The left fist on the left hip.

【Feet】
Left-Kokutsudachi.

【Hands】
Same as in ㊴.

【Feet】
Cross left foot in front.

【Note】
Do not change the position of the hands when sliding the left foot.
Move the left foot slowly.

【Hands】
Pull the right fist towards the left shoulder. Keep the left fist is place.

【Feet】
Excute a Right-Chudan-Mae-Geri. Stand on the left leg.

【Note】
The pulling of the right fist and the Maegeri are done simultaneously.

相手に手首をつかまれた時、つかまれた腕は動かさないで、後足を前足に交差させ、適切な間合いをとり中段蹴りで反撃するとともに、つかまれた腕を肩口に引く。相手がさらに下段突きで反撃した場合、下段突き、中段突きで攻撃、上段突きで反撃した場合は、上段揚げ受けをする。

When an opponent grabs the wrist, do not move the grabbed arm, cross the back leg over the front leg, take an appropriate distance and counterattack with a Chudan-geri, and pull the grabbed arm towards the shoulder. If the opponent further counterattacks with a Gedan-Zuki, attack with Gedan-Zuki, Chudan-Zuki. If the opponent counterattacks with an Jodan-Zuki, then deflect with and Jodan-Age-Uke.

挙動 35	挙動 36	挙動 37	途中
 ❺⓻	 ❺⓼	 ❺⓽	 ❻⓪
後ろ	 後ろ	 後ろ	

【手の動作】
右拳下段突き（甲上向き）。左拳はそのまま。

【足の動作】
右足を左足前におろし、右足前半月立ち。

【手の動作】
左中段逆突き。右拳右腰に引く。

【足の動作】
立ち方はそのまま。

【留意点】
腰を右に回転する。

【手の動作】
右上段揚げ受け。左拳左腰に引く。

【足の動作】
立ち方はそのまま。

【手の動作】
左拳は右腰前から額前上を弧を描いてゆっくり縦に回す。右拳右腰に引く。

【足の動作】
左足裏を右膝横に引きつけ、左膝をかい込む。

【留意点】
左拳、左足は揃えてゆっくり。顔は南を向く。

【Hands】
Execute a Gedan-Zuki with the right fist (Kou is upward). Keep the left fist is place.

【Feet】
Drop the right foot in front of the left foot, into Right-Hangetsudachi.

【Hands】
Execute a Left-Chudan-Gyaku-Zuki. Pull the right fist back to the right hip.

【Feet】
Same as in ❺⓻.

【Note】
Rotate the hips to the right.

【Hands】
Execute a Right-Jodan-Age-Uke. Pull the left fist back to the left hip.

【Feet】
Same as in ❺⓻.

【Hands】
Slowly rotate the left fist vertically in an arc from in front of the right hip to above the forehead. Pull the right fist to the right hip.

【Feet】
Pull the sole of the left foot to the side of the right knee while tucking the knee in.

【Note】
Maintain simultaneous slow movement with the left fist and left foot. Turn the face to the south.

【Hands】
Execute a Gedan-Zuki with the left fist (Kou is upward). Keep the right fist is place.

【Feet】
Drop the left foot in front of the right foot, into Left-Hangetsudachi.

途中

(61)

【足の動作】
ゆっくり腰を左に回転しながら、左足を弧を描いて回し、南へつま先からおろす。

【Feet】
While slowly rotating the hips to the left, rotate the left foot in an arc and bring it down to the south, landing first on the toe.

挙動 38

(62)

【手の動作】
左裏拳縦回し打ち。右拳右腰。

【足の動作】
右後屈立ち。

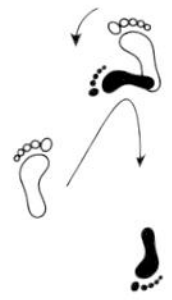

【Hands】
Excute a Left-Uraken-Tate-Mawashi-Uchi.

【Feet】
Right-Kokutsudachi.

挙動 39

(63)

【手の動作】
左拳開掌（甲左向き）。右拳はそのまま。

【足の動作】
右足の足底を左掌に当てて、右中段三日月蹴り。左脚立ち。

【Hands】
Open the left fist (Kou is leftward). Keep the right fist is place.

【Feet】
Execute a Right-Chudan-Mikazuki-Geri. The sole of the right foot is kicked against the left palm. Stand on the left leg.

挙動 40

(64)

【手の動作】
右中段逆突き（低め）。左拳左腰に引く。

【足の動作】
右足を北へ引き、左足前半月立ち。

【留意点】
挙動 39 ～ 40 は連続する。
気合い。

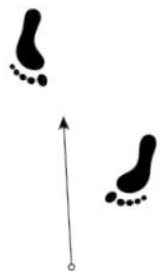

【Hands】
Execute a Right-Chudan-Gyaku-Zuki (low). Pull the left fist back to the left hip.

【Feet】
Pull right leg back toward the north into Left-Hangetsudachi.

【Note】
(63) and (64) are continuous.
Kiai.

途中	挙動41	途中	止め

⑥⑤	⑥⑥	⑥⑦	⑥⑧

【手の動作】
ゆっくり両掌を両腰に引く（両掌前向き）。

【足の動作】
右足を北へ少し引き下げる。

【手の動作】
両掌底下段合わせ受け（両掌を押し出し掌底を合わせる）。

【足の動作】
左足を引き、左足前猫足立ち。

【手の動作】
左右の拳を握り胸前で交差。

【足の動作】
右足の位置はそのまま、左足をもどす。

【手の動作】
両拳を大腿部前に持っていく。

【足の動作】
八字立ち。

【Hands】
Slowly pull both palms toward the hips (Both Hira are forward).

【Feet】
Draw the right foot slightly toward the north.

【Hands】
Execute a Gedan-Awase-Uke with both Shotei (heel of palms). Push both palms out and bring the Shotei together.

【Feet】
Pull the left leg, into Left-Nekoashidachi.

【Hands】
Clench the left and right fists and cross them in front of the chest.

【Feet】
Bring the left foot back, leaving the right foot in the same position.

【Hands】
Place both fists in front of the thighs.

【Feet】
Hachijidachi.

相手の中段前蹴りを、猫足立ちになりながら両掌底で受ける。
As the opponent performs a Chudan-Mae-Geri, deflect it with the both Shotei while in the Nekoashidachi stance.

挙動の解釈 Application (Bunkai) of ⑥⑤

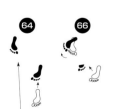

挙動40で北へ寄り足をして左足前半月立ちになり、その後挙動41で左足の位置を変え左足前猫足立ちになる方法もある。

挙動の解釈 Application of ⑥④ to ⑥⑥

直立	礼	直立

⑥⑨	⑦⓪	⑦①

【手の動作】
両手は開いて大腿部両側に付けて伸ばす。

【足の動作】
結び立ち。

礼をする。

【手の動作】
手はそのまま。

【足の動作】
足はそのまま。

【Hands】
Open both hands and extend them down along the sides of the thighs.

【Feet】
Musubidachi.

＊ Bow (Rei).

【Hands】
Same as in ⑥⑨.

【Feet】
Same as in ⑥⑨.

Another method is to step the north in movement 40 and make Hangetsudachi stance on the left foot in the front, then change the position of the left foot in movement 41 and make Nekoashidachi stance with the left foot in the front.

十手
Jitte
（24挙動）

この形は習熟すれば十人の働きをするという意味で名付けられたといわれている。比較的短い形ではあるが重厚な形である。この形の特徴は棒の攻撃への攻防にある。棒を両手でつかみ取り上げたり、受けたあと捻ったり、相手の逆をとったりする技が含まれている。

It is said that the kata of this Jitte (ten hands) was named in the sense that it will work as ten people if it is mastered. Although it is a relatively short kata, it is a profound kata. The characteristic of this kata is the attack and defense against Bo's attack, including the techniques of grabbing Bo with both hands, taking it up, twisting it after guarding it, and taking the opposite side of opponent.

十手　挙動一覧

十手　各挙動解説

直立	礼	直立	用意
 ❶	 ❷	 ❸	 ❹

❶
【手の動作】
両手は開いて大腿部両側につけて伸ばす。

【足の動作】
結び立ち（左右とも正面に対して約30度）。

❷
礼をする。

❸
【手の動作】
手はそのまま。

【足の動作】
立ち方はそのまま。

❹
【手の動作】
右拳を左掌で包み、下顎前に構える。両肘の間隔は肩幅程度。

【足の動作】
結び立ちから閉足立ちになる。

【Hands】
Open both hands and extend them down along the sides of the thighs.

【Feet】
Musubidachi.

* Bow (Rei).

【Hands】
Same as in ❶.

【Feet】
Same as in ❶.

【Hands】
Wrapping right fist with left palm, hold hands in front of lower part of jaw about two fists distance away. Space between both elbows is about shoulder width.

【Feet】
Move from Musubidachi to Heisokudachi.

* Explanation of terms in the text.
　Kou : The back of the hand
　Hira : The palm of the hand

挙動の解釈 Application (Bunkai) of ❹ - ❽

| 途中 | 挙動1 | 途中 | 挙動2 |

【手の動作】
左掌を軽く顔の前に出し、縦に回して下に。右拳は開いて胸から顎前をとおり前方へ縦に弧を描くように回す。

【足の動作】
左足を北に引く。

【留意点】
右掌は五指を浅く曲げる（甲下向き）。ゆっくり力を入れる。

【手の動作】
右手背手首中段押さえ受け。左拳左腰に引く。

【足の動作】
右前屈立ち。

【留意点】
両手と左足はゆっくり同時に。

【手の動作】
右掌底を裏返しながら下へ（甲上向き）、左拳を開掌し、下から左掌底を左肩前に。

【足の動作】
左足を南東へすり出す。

【手の動作】
左掌底中段押し上げ受け。右掌底中段押し下げ受け。

【足の動作】
左前屈立ち。

【留意点】
ゆっくりと力を入れる。

【Hands】
Gently bring the left palm out in front of the face, turn it vertically and point it down. Open the right fist and rotate it in a vertical arc from the chest to the chin.

【Feet】
Pull the left leg back toward the north.

【Note】
The five fingers of the right palm are slightly bent (Kou is down). Apply pressure slowly.

【Hands】
Execute a Chudan-Osae-Uke with the back of the right wrist. Pull left fist to left hip.

【Feet】
Right-Zenkutsudachi.

【Note】
Both hands and left foot move slowly and simultaneously.

【Hands】
Flip the bottom of the right palm downwards (Kou is up), open the left fist, and from its current position bring it in front of the left shoulder.

【Feet】
Slide the left foot the south east.

【Hands】
Execute a Left-Chudan-Oshiage-Uke with a Shoutei. Execute a Right-Chudan-Oshisage-Uke with a Shotei.

【Feet】
Left-Zenkutsudachi.

【Note】
Make sure to slowly exert force with the hands

相手が棒で突いてきたとき、右手首で棒を上から押さえる。続いて右掌を返して棒をつかみ左掌で押しこむ。

When the opponent attacks with a Bo, press down the Bo from above with the right wrist.
Next, turn the right palm, grab the Bo, and push it in with the left palm.

挙動3	挙動4	途中	挙動5
⑨	⑩	⑪	⑫

【手の動作】
右手はそのまま。左前腕を右に倒して、四指を伸ばし左掌中段押さえ受け（甲上向き）。

【足の動作】
立ち方はそのまま。

【留意点】
顔は西を向く。

【手の動作】
右掌手首右側面中段掛け受け（甲下向き）。左拳左腰に引く。

【足の動作】
西へ半歩寄り足をし、騎馬立ち。

【手の動作】
左拳はそのまま。右掌は腰の回転に合わせて右側方から横に回す。

【足の動作】
左足を半歩西へ引き寄せながら左脚を軸に腰を左回転する。

【留意点】
右掌は肘をやや曲げる。

【手の動作】
右掌底右側面中段横受け。左拳はそのまま。

【足の動作】
騎馬立ち。

北 North
西 West　東 East
南 South

【Hands】
Keep the right hand as is. Tilt the left forearm to the right, extend the four fingers, and execute a Chudan-Osae-Uke with the left palm (Kou is up).

【Feet】
Same as in ⑧.

【Note】
Turn the face to the west.

【Hands】
Execute a Chudan-Kake-Uke (Kou is down) to the right side with the right palm wrist. Pull the left fist to the left hip.

【Feet】
Slide (Yoriashi) a little to the west into a Kibadachi.

【Hands】
Keep the left fist as is. Rotate the right palm along with the right-side hip rotation, and turn from the right side.

【Feet】
Rotate the hips to the left with the left leg as the axis while pulling the left foot half a step to the west.

【Note】
The right elbow is slightly bent.

【Hands】
Execute a Chudan-Yoko-Uke on the right side with the right Shotei. The left fist remains in place.

【Feet】
Kibadachi.

相手の左中段突きの手首を右掌底で押し下げながら、左掌底を相手の顎に打ち付ける。
While pushing down the opponent's left Chudan-zuki with the right Shotei, strike with the bottom of the left Shotei the opponent's chin.

挙動の解釈 Application (Bunkai) of ⑧

【手の動作】
左掌底左側面中段横受け。右拳は右腰に引く。

【足の動作】
右脚を軸に左足を南へ1歩進め、騎馬立ち。

【手の動作】
右掌底右側面中段横受け。左拳は左腰に引く。

【足の動作】
左脚を軸に右足を南へ1歩進め、騎馬立ち。

【手の動作】
両拳上段交差受け（右手外）。

【足の動作】
右足前交差立ち。

【手の動作】
両拳両側下段打ち払い（両甲外向き）。

【足の動作】
北へ半歩寄り足し、騎馬立ち。

【Hands】
Execute a Chudan-Yoko-Uke on the left side with the left Shotei. The right fist is pulled back to the right hip.

【Feet】
Take one step to the south with the right leg as the axis, and stand into a Kibadachi.

【Hands】
Execute a Chudan-Yoko-Uke on the right side with the right Shotei. The left fist is pulled back to the left hip.

【Feet】
Take one step to the south with the left leg as the axis, and stand into a Kibadachi.

【Hands】
Execute a Jodan-Kosa-Uke with both fists (right fist in front).

【Feet】
With the right foot in front, into a Kousadachi.

【Hands】
Execute a Gedan-Uchi-Barai on both sides with both fists (Both Kou are outward).

【Feet】
Slide (Yoriashi) a little to the north into a Kibadachi.

挙動の解釈 Application (Bunkai) of ⑬ - ⑭

騎馬立ちで左掌底で側面から棒を払う。さらに左掌でつかみながら右足を前に出し、左掌底で相手の中段を攻撃する。

Stand in a Kibadachi and deflect the Bo from the side with the bottom of the left palm. In addition, move the right foot forward while grasping the Bo with the left palm, then attack to the Chudan of the opponent with the right Shotei.

挙動 10	途中	途中	挙動 11

⑰	⑱	⑲	⑳

横	横	横	

【手の動作】
両拳を胸前で交差させ、かき分けながら左右上段に開き、山構え（上段掻き分け受け）。

【足の動作】
騎馬立ちのまま、さらに北へ寄り足。

【手の動作】
両手はそのまま。

【足の動作】
立ち方はそのまま。

【留意点】
顔は南を向く。

【手の動作】
両手はそのまま。

【足の動作】
左膝を曲げたまま高く左胸前にかい込む。

【手の動作】
左前腕左側面上段打ち払い。

【足の動作】
左足を踏み込んで騎馬立ち。

【留意点】
右脚を軸に腰を右回転する。

【Hands】
Execute a Jodan-Kakiwake-Uke. Cross both fists in front of the chest, with Kakiwake (dividing/splitting motion) reaching the upper of both sides and ending in a Yama-Gamae (mountain posture with hands).

【Feet】
While maintaining the position in a Kibadachi, move further north.

【Hands】
Same as in ⑰.

【Feet】
Same as in ⑰.

【Note】
Turn the face to the south.

【Hands】
Same as in ⑱.

【Feet】
Keeping the left knee bent, pull it up high in front of the left chest.

【Hands】
Execute a Jodan-Uchi-Barai on the left side with the left forearm.

【Feet】
Stomp down with the left foot and stand into a Kibadachi.

【Note】
Rotate the hips right around the axis of the right leg.

【手の動作】
両手はそのまま。

【足の動作】
右膝を曲げたまま高く右胸前にかい込む。

【手の動作】
右前腕右側面上段打ち払い。

【足の動作】
右足を踏み込んで騎馬立ち。

【留意点】
左脚を軸に腰を左回転する。

【手の動作】
両手はそのまま。

【足の動作】
左膝を曲げたまま高く左胸前にかい込む。

【手の動作】
左前腕左側面上段打ち払い。

【足の動作】
左足を踏み込んで騎馬立ち。

【留意点】
右脚を軸に腰を右回転する。
気合い。
挙動11〜13は顔を南を向いたまま山構えの姿勢を崩さず、腰の回転に合わせて向きを変える。

【Hands】
Same as in ⑳.

【Feet】
Keeping the right knee bent, pull it up high in front of the right chest.

【Hands】
Execute a Jodan-Uchi-Barai on the right side with the right forearm.

【Feet】
Stomp down with the right foot and stand into a Kibadachi.

【Note】
Rotate the hips left around the axis of the left leg.

【Hands】
Same as in ㉒.

【Feet】
Keeping the left knee bent, pull it up high in front of the left chest.

【Hands】
Execute a Jodan-Uchi-Barai on the left side with the left forearm.

【Feet】
Stomp down with the left foot and stand into a Kibadachi.

【Note】
Rotate the hips right around the axis of the right leg.
Kiai.
From movement 11 to 13 maintain Yama-Gamae posture with the face facing south, and change direction as the hips rotate.

途中	挙動 14	挙動 15	挙動 16
㉕	㉖ 	㉗ 	㉘ 
	横	後ろ	後ろ

【手の動作】
ゆっくりと両腕を胸前で交差する。

【足の動作】
ゆっくり膝を伸ばし、右足を左足に寄せる。

【手の動作】
両拳両側に掻き分け。

【足の動作】
八字立ち。

【留意点】
両拳をゆっくり掻き分け下ろしながら、顔を北へ向ける。

【手の動作】
右拳を開手し、右手刀右側面上段横受け。左拳は左腰に引く。

【足の動作】
左脚を軸に右足を北へすり出し、右前屈立ち。

【手の動作】
右掌を下段に下げ、右掌のあった位置へ左掌を押し出し、両掌虎口棒受け。

【足の動作】
立ち方はそのまま。

【留意点】
右肘は少し曲げる。
両掌とも虎口を北向きに上下一直線に並べる。

北 North
西 West — 東 East
南 South

【Hands】
Cross the arms in front of the chest slowly.

【Feet】
Straighten the knees slowly and slide the right foot towards the left foot.

【Hands】
Extend both fists to the sides of the body (Kakiwake).

【Feet】
Hachijidachi.

【Note】
Lower both fists slowly (Kakiwake) while turning the face to the north.

【Hands】
Right fist open, execute a Jodan-Yoko-Uke on right side with right Shuto. Left fist pulled to left hip.

【Feet】
With the left leg as the axis, the right foot slides out to the north into a Right-Zenkutsudachi.

【Hands】
Lower the right palm into Gedan, push the left palm out to where the right palm was, and execute a Ko-Kou-Bo-Uke with both palms.

【Feet】
Same as in ㉗.

【Note】
The right elbow is slightly bent. Both palms should be aligned vertically in a straight line with the Ko-kou facing north.

挙動の解釈 Application (Bunkai) of ㉕ - ㉘

挙動 17-1	挙動 17-2	挙動 18-1	挙動 18-2

横	後ろ	横	後ろ

【手の動作】
右掌は右肩上に（甲後ろ向き）、左掌は右脇に（甲前向き）両虎口を上下一直線に並べる。

【足の動作】
左膝を前にかい込み、左足を右膝に添える。右脚立ち。

【手の動作】右掌上段押し出し、左掌下段押し出し（両虎口は前向き）。

【足の動作】左足を踏み出し寄り足して左前屈立ち。

【留意点】両掌とも虎口を北向きに上下一直線に並べる。

【手の動作】
左掌は左肩上に（甲後ろ向き）、右掌は左脇に（甲前向き）両虎口を上下一直線に並べる。

【足の動作】
右膝を前にかい込み、右足を左膝に添える。左脚立ち。

【手の動作】左掌上段押し出し、右掌下段押し出し（両虎口は前向き）。

【足の動作】右足を踏み出し寄り足して右前屈立ち。

【留意点】両掌とも虎口を北向きに上下一直線に並べる。

【Hands】
The right palm is positioned above the right shoulder (Kou is backward), and the left palm is positioned by the right side (Kou is forward), align both Ko-kou in a straight line vertically.

【Feet】
Lift up the left knee in front of the body and put the left foot on the right knee. Standing on the right leg.

【Hands】
Excute a Jodan-Oshidashi with the right palm, Gedan-Oshidashi with the left palm. (Both Ko-kou are facing forward).

【Feet】
Step and thrust forward with the left foot, and finish in a Zenkutsudachi.

【Note】
Both palms should be aligned vertically in a straight line with the Ko-kou facing north.

【Hands】
The left palm is positioned above the left shoulder (Kou is backward), and the right palm is positioned by the left side (Kou is forward), align both Ko-kou in a straight line vertically.

【Feet】
Lift up the right knee in front of the body and put the right foot on the left knee. Standing on the left leg.

【Hands】
Excute a Jodan-Oshidashi with the left palm, Gedan-Oshidashi with the right palm. (Both Ko-kou are facing forward).

【Feet】
Step and thrust forward with the right foot, and finish in a Zenkutsudachi.

【Note】
Both palms should be aligned vertically in a straight line with the Ko-kou facing north.

相手が棒を頭上から打ち込んできたとき、右手刀で受け、手首を返して棒をつかみ、右手を肘を中心にして押し下げる。

When the opponent attacks with a Bo from above the head, receive it with the right Shuto, then rotate the wrist, grab the Bo, and push down with the right hand centered on the elbow.

挙動の解釈 Application (Bunkai) of ㉙ - ㉜

相手が棒で打ち込んできた場合、両掌で受け、脇腹を締めながら手首を返して棒をつかみとる。

If the opponent strikes with the Bo, catch it with both palms, and while tightening both sides, turn the wrists and grab the Bo.

| 途中 | 挙動 19 | 途中 | 挙動 20 |

【手の動作】
両拳開掌。両腕をいったん胸前で交差する。

【足の動作】
右脚を軸に体を左に回転させ、左足を東に移す。

【手の動作】
右拳右側面上段受け、左拳左側面下段受け。

【足の動作】
右後屈立ち。

【手の動作】
西に振り向きながら両拳開掌。両腕をいったん胸前で交差する。

【足の動作】
方向を西に変え、左脚に軸を移す。

【手の動作】
左拳左側面上段受け。右拳右側面下段受け。

【足の動作】
左後屈立ち。

【Hands】
Open both hands so they are flat and immediately cross the arms in front of the chest.

【Feet】
With the right leg as the axis, turn the body to the left and bring left foot to the east.

【Hands】
Execute a Right-Jodan-Uke with the right fist and a Left-Gedan-Uke with the left fist.

【Feet】
Right-Kokutsudachi.

【Hands】
Turn to the west and open both fists. Cross both arms once in front of the chest.

【Feet】
Change the direction to the west and move the axis to the left leg.

【Hands】
Execute a Left-Jodan-Uke with the left fist and a Right-Gedan-Uke with the right fist.

【Feet】
Left-Kokutsudachi.

【手の動作】
右拳は開掌し額前に上げる。左拳は左腰に引く。

【足の動作】
右足の位置はそのままにして、左足を南へすり出す。

【手の動作】
左上段揚げ受け。右拳は右腰に引く。

【足の動作】
左前屈立ち。

【手の動作】
左拳開掌。右拳はそのまま。

【足の動作】
右足を南へ一歩進める。

【手の動作】
右上段揚げ受け。左拳は左腰に引く。

【足の動作】
右前屈立ち。

【Hands】
Right fist open and raised in front of forehead. The left fist pulls back to the left hip.

【Feet】
Leave the right foot in place and slide the left foot out to the south.

【Hands】
Execute a Left-Jodan-Age-Uke. Pull the right fist back to the right hip.

【Feet】
Left-Zenkutsudachi.

【Hands】
Left fist open. The right fist remains in place.

【Feet】
Advance right foot toward south.

【Hands】
Execute a Right-Jodan-Age-Uke. Pull the left fist back to the left hip.

【Feet】
Right-Zenkutsudachi.

途中	挙動23	途中	挙動24

後ろ	後ろ	後ろ	後ろ

【手の動作】
右拳は開掌し額前に上げる。左拳は左腰に引く。

【足の動作】
右脚を軸に体を左回転し、左足を北に移す。

【手の動作】
左上段揚げ受け。右拳は右腰に引く。

【足の動作】
左前屈立ち。

【留意点】
挙動22～23は連続する。

【手の動作】
左拳開掌。右拳はそのまま。

【足の動作】
右足を北へ一歩進める。

【手の動作】
右上段揚げ受け。左拳は左腰に引く。

【足の動作】
右前屈立ち。

【留意点】
気合い。

【Hands】
Right fist open and raised in front of the forehead. Pull the left palm back to the left hip.

【Feet】
With the right leg as the axis, rotate hips to the left and slide the left foot to the north.

【Hands】
Execute a Left-Jodan-Age-Uke. Pull the right fist back to the right hip.

【Feet】
Left-Zenkutsudachi.

【Note】
㊵ to ㊷ are continuous.

【Hands】
Left fist open. The right fist remains in place.

【Feet】
Advance the right foot toward to the north.

【Hands】
Execute a Right-Jodan-Age-Uke. Pull the left fist back to the left hip.

【Feet】
Right-Zenkutsudachi.

【Note】
Kiai.

止め	直立	礼	直立

㊺	㊻	㊼	㊽

【手の動作】
右拳を左掌で包み下顎前に構え、用意の姿勢に戻る。

【足の動作】
右脚を軸に左回りに回転しながら、左足を右足に引きつけ、閉足立ち。

【手の動作】
両手は開いて大腿部両側に付けて伸ばす。

【足の動作】
結び立ち。

礼をする。

【手の動作】
手はそのまま。

【足の動作】
足はそのまま。

【Hands】
Wrapping right fist with left hand, position both hands in front of jaw before returning to 'Yoi' position.

【Feet】
While rotating leftward with right leg as axis, pull the left foot to the right foot into a Heisokudachi.

【Hands】
Open both hands and extend them down along the sides of the thighs.

【Feet】
Musubidachi.

＊ Bow (Rei).

【Hands】
Same as in ㊻.

【Feet】
Same as in ㊻.

珍手
Chinte
（32 挙動）

この形は、基本技では比較的珍しい技が含まれている。不動立ちより前屈立ちに変化させながら縦拳を使用して突く技、人差し指と中指での二本貫手で眼を攻撃する技、さらに背刀下段回し受け、中高一本拳中段打ち落としなどの技である。また最後の挙動の縦突きの後、すり足で下がるときは、砂浜で波が引くような気持で演武しなければならないといわれている。前屈立ち、不動立ち、後屈立ち、騎馬立ちの使い分けを意識しながら体得しなければならない。

This kata contains a basic but relatively unusual technique. These include Tsuki techniques using Tate-ken while changing from Fudodachi to Zenkutsudachi, Nihon-Nukite with the index and middle fingers to attack the eyes, and techniques such as Haito-Gedan-Mawashi-Uke, Naka-Daka-Ippon-Ken-Chudan-Uchiotoshi. It is also said that after the final movement of Tate-Zuki, when the students descend in Suri-Ashi, they must perform as if they were waves receding on a sandy beach. The use of Zenkutsudachi, Fudodachi, Kokutsudachi, and Kibadachi must be learned and practiced with awareness.

珍手　挙動一覧

礼	直立

珍手　各挙動解説

直立	礼	直立	用意

❶	❷	❸	❹

【手の動作】
両手は開いて大腿部両側につけて伸ばす。

【足の動作】
結び立ち（左右とも正面に対して約30度）。

礼をする。

【手の動作】
手はそのまま。

【足の動作】
立ち方はそのまま。

【手の動作】
水月前で左拳（甲下向き）の上に右拳（甲前向き）を重ねて構える。

【足の動作】
閉足立ち。

【Hands】
Open both hands and extend them down along the sides of the thighs.

【Feet】
Musubidachi (left and right feet are angled approximately 30 degrees from the front).

∗ Bow (Rei).

【Hands】
Same as in ❶.

【Feet】
Same as in ❶.

【Hands】
Place the left fist in front of the solar plexus (Kou is down), and place the right fist on top of the left fist (Kou is forward).

【Feet】
Move from a Musubidachi to a Heisokudachi.

∗ Explanation of terms in the text.
　Kou : The back of the hand
　Hira : The palm of the hand

❺ 途中	❻ 挙動1	❼ 途中	❽ 途中

【手の動作】
右拳槌を額前より西へ高く縦に回す。左拳はそのまま。

【足の動作】
立ち方はそのまま

【留意点】
顔は西を向く。ゆっくり力を入れる。

【手の動作】
右拳槌中段縦回し打ち。左拳はそのまま。

【足の動作】
立ち方はそのまま。

【手の動作】
右拳槌を左拳の下に戻す（甲下向き）。左拳を縦にする（甲前向き）。

【足の動作】
立ち方はそのまま。

【留意点】
顔は東を向く。

【手の動作】
左拳槌を額前より東へ高く縦に回す。右拳はそのまま。

【足の動作】
立ち方はそのまま。

【留意点】
ゆっくり力を入れる。

【Hands】
Turn the right Kentsui from the forehead to the west vertically upwards. Retain the left fist in its position.

【Feet】
Same as in ❷.

【Note】
Turn the face to the west. Move Kentsui slowly exert force.

【Hands】
Execute a Chudan-Tate-Mawashi-Uchi with right Kentsui. The left fist remains in place.

【Feet】
Same as in ❷.

【Hands】
Return the right Kentsui and place it beneath the left fist. (Right Kou is down and Left Kou is forward).

【Feet】
Same as in ❷.

【Note】
Turn the face to the east.

【Hands】
Turn the left Kentsui from the forehead to the east vertically upwards. Retain the right fist in its position.

【Feet】
Same as in ❷.

【Note】
Slowly exert force.

相手の中段突きを拳槌で叩き落す。

Knock down the opponent's Chudan-Zuki with Kentsui(hammer- fist).

挙動の解釈 Application (Bunkai) of ❻

| 挙動2 | 挙動3 | 途中 | 挙動4 |

【手の動作】
左拳槌中段縦回し打ち。右拳はそのまま。

【足の動作】
立ち方はそのまま。

【留意点】
挙動1、2はゆっくり力を入れて一呼吸で。

【手の動作】
両手指先を合わせて額前に上げて、両掌上段揚げ受け。

【足の動作】
右脚を軸に腰を右転し左足を南へすり出し、騎馬立ち。

【留意点】
顔は西を向く。

【手の動作】
左拳を右肩前に出すとともに、右掌を左脇下からゆっくり大きく弧を描き前に出す。

【足の動作】
左脚を軸に右足を東へ移す。

【手の動作】
右中段縦手刀受け、左拳は左腰に引く。

【足の動作】
右足前不動立ち。

【留意点】
ゆっくり。

【Hands】
Execute a Chudan-Tate-Mawashi-Uchi with left Kentsui. The right fist remains in place.

【Feet】
Same as in ❷.

【Hands】
Bring the fingertips of both hands together and raise them in front of the forehead.
Then, execute a Jodan-Age-Uke with both hands.

【Feet】
Rotate the hips to the right with the right leg as the axis, slide the left foot to the south, and stand in Kibadachi.

【Note】
Turn the face to the west.

【Hands】
Extend left fist in front of right shoulder, and draw out a large arc from below the left armpit to the front with open right hand.

【Feet】
With the left leg as the axis, move the right foot to the east.

【Hands】
Execute a Right-Chudan-Tate-Shuto-Uke. Pull back left fist to the left hip.

【Feet】
Right-Fudodachi.

【Note】
Do slowly.

相手の上段攻撃を手刀で受ける。

Deflect the opponent's upper-level attack with the Shuto(sword-hand).

挙動の解釈 Application (Bunkai) of ⓾

挙動5	途中	挙動6	挙動7

 後ろ	 後ろ	後ろ	 後ろ

【手の動作】
右掌に左中段縦突き。

【足の動作】
右前屈立ち。

【留意点】
素早く突く。

【手の動作】
右拳を左肩前に出すとともに、左掌を右脇下からゆっくり大きく弧を描き前に出す。

【足の動作】
左足を北へすり出す。

【留意点】
左足、左手同時にゆっくり。

【手の動作】
左中段縦手刀受け。右拳は右腰に引く。

【足の動作】
左足前不動立ち。

【留意点】
ゆっくり。

【手の動作】
左掌に右中段縦突き。

【足の動作】
左前屈立ち。

【留意点】
素早く突く。

【Hands】
Execute a Left Chudan-Tate-Zuki to the right palm.

【Feet】
Right-Zenkutsudachi.

【Note】
Do fast.

【Hands】
Extend right fist in front of left shoulder, and draw out a large arc from below the right armpit to the front with open left hand.

【Feet】
Slide the left foot to the north.

【Note】
Left foot and left hand move slowly and simultaneously.

【Hands】
Execute a Left-Chudan-Tate-Shuto-Uke. Pull back right fist to the right hip.

【Feet】
Left-Fudodachi.

【Note】
Do slowly.

【Hands】
Execute a Right Chudan-Tate-Zuki to the left palm.

【Feet】
Left-Zenkutsudachi.

【Note】
Do fast.

途中	挙動8	挙動9	挙動10

 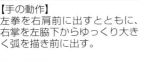 後ろ	 後ろ	 後ろ	

【手の動作】
左拳を右肩前に出すとともに、右掌を左脇下からゆっくり大きく弧を描き前に出す。

【足の動作】
右足を北へすり出す。

【留意点】
ゆっくり。

【手の動作】
右中段縦手刀受け。左拳は左腰に引く。

【足の動作】
右足前不動立ち。

【手の動作】
右掌に左上段縦猿臂打ち。

【足の動作】
右前屈立ち。

【留意点】
縦猿臂は腰を入れる。
気合い。

【手の動作】
左手刀中段受け、右手刀胸前。

【足の動作】
右脚を軸にして腰を左転し、南へ向きを変え、右後屈立ち。

【留意点】
挙動9～10は連続する。

【Hands】
Extend left fist in front of right shoulder, and draw out a large arc from below the left armpit to the front with open right hand.

【Feet】
Slide the right foot to the north.

【Note】
Do slowly.

【Hands】
Execute a Right-Chudan-Tate-Shuto-Uke. Pull back left fist to the left hip.

【Feet】
Right-Fudodachi.

【Hands】
Execute a Left-Jodan-Tate-Enpi-Uchi. The left elbow must strike and be placed against the right palm.

【Feet】
Right-Zenkutsudachi.

【Note】
Twist the hips for the Tate-Enpi.
Kiai

【Hands】
Execute a Left-Shuto-Chudan-Uke. Hold Right-Shuto in front of the chest.

【Feet】
Rotate the hips to the left with the right leg as axis, and turn the face to the south, into a Right-Kokutsudachi.

【Note】
⑲ and ⑳ are continuous.

 挙動 11
 挙動 12
 途中
 挙動 13

【手の動作】
右手刀中段受け、左手刀胸前。

【足の動作】
右足を南へ一歩進め、左後屈立ち。

【手の動作】
手はそのまま。

【足の動作】
左中段前蹴り、右脚立ち。

【留意点】
後屈立ちのままの位置から南へ前蹴り。

【手の動作】
両手を握り、左拳は右肩前、右拳は左脇腹へ持っていく。

【足の動作】
左前蹴りを北へ引く。

【手の動作】
右中段外受け、左下段受け。

【足の動作】
左足を後ろに下ろし右前屈立ち。

【留意点】
挙動12～13は連続する。蹴り足の着地と受けは同時にする。

【Hands】
Execute a Right-Shuto-Chudan-Uke. Hold Left-Shuto in front of the chest.

【Feet】
Take right foot one step toward south into a Left-Kokutsudachi.

【Hands】
Same as in ㉑.

【Feet】
Execute a Left-Chudan-Mae-Geri. Stand on the right leg.

【Note】
Execute a Mae-Geri to the south from where Koukutsudachi remains.

【Hands】
Hold both hands closed, take the left fist to the front of the right shoulder, and the right fist to the left side (close to the armpit).

【Feet】
Pull the left Mae-Geri to the north.

【Hands】
Execute a Right-Chudan-Soto-Uke, and a Left-Gedan-Uke.

【Feet】
Right-Zenkutsudachi.

【Note】
㉒ to ㉔ are continuous. Kicking leg landing and the Uke are simultaneous.

【手の動作】
右手首を返しながら甲前向きで下段を受け、大きく弧を描いて頭上から下段へ回す（甲下向き）。左拳は左腰に引く。

【手の動作】
右下段すくい受け（甲下向き）。左拳はそのまま。

【足の動作】
右足に左足を引きつけ閉足立ち。

【手の動作】
両拳を開掌し、両手同時に軽く伸ばし、左から右へ大きな弧を描くように振り回す。

【足の動作】
右足を北へすり出す。

【Hands】
Turn the right wrist downward to execute a Gedan-Uke (Kou is forward), continue rotating the fist in a large arc over the head and then turn it down in a Gedan-Uke block to the Gedan (Kou is downward). Pull the left fist toward the left hip.

【Hands】
Execute a Right-Sukui-Uke (Kou is down). Keep the left fist as it is.

【Feet】
Pull the left foot to the right foot and stand in Heisokudachi.

【Hands】
Open both fists, lightly stretching out the fingers of both hands at the same time, and swing them in a large arc from left to right.

【Feet】
Slide the right foot to the north.

挙動の解釈 Application (Bunkai) of ㉕ - ㉗

相手の蹴りを右手ですくいながら受ける。

Deflect the opponent's kick by scooping and swinging it away with the right hand.

【手の動作】
左背刀下段回し受け。右手刀水月前構え。

【足の動作】
北へ寄り足しながら騎馬立ち。

【手の動作】
両手同時に軽く伸ばし、右から左へ大きな弧を描くように振り回す。

【Hands】
Execute a Gedan-Mawashi-Uke with left Haitou. Right Shuto held in front of solar plexus.

【Feet】
Slide (Yoriashi) a little to the north in a Kibadachi.

【Hands】
Lightly stretching out the fingers of both hands at the same time, and swing them in a large arc from right to left.

【手の動作】
右背刀下段回し受け。左手刀水月前構え。

【手の動作】
両拳を胸前で交差する。

【足の動作】
騎馬立ちのまま南へ寄り足。

【Hands】
Execute a Gedan-Mawashi-Uke with right Haitou. Left Shuto held in front of solar plexus.

【Feet】
Slide (Yoriashi) a little to the south, keeping the Kibadachi.

【Hands】
Cross the arms in front of the chest.

| 挙動17 | 途中 | 途中 | 挙動18 |

【手の動作】
両拳中段掻き分け受け。

【足の動作】
騎馬立ちのまま南へ寄り足。

【留意点】
挙動16〜17は連続する。

【手の動作】
ゆっくり両腕を胸前で交差する。

【足の動作】
右足甲を左膝裏に添える。

【手の動作】
両拳両側に掻き分け。

【足の動作】
左脚立ち。

【Hands】
Execute a Chudan-Kakiwake-Uke with both fists.

【Feet】
Slide (Yoriashi) a little to the south, keeping the Kibadachi.

【Note】
㉟ to ㊲ are continuous.

【Hands】
Cross the arms in front of the chest slowly.

【Feet】
Place the front of the right foot on the back of the left knee.

【Hands】
Extend both fists to the sides of the body (Kakiwake).

【Feet】
Stand on the left leg.

【手の動作】 右腕を少し伸ばして右中高一本拳を上から振り下ろす（甲上向き）。 【足の動作】 右足を西へおろす。	【手の動作】 右中高一本拳中段打ち落とし。左拳は左腰に引く。 【足の動作】 右前屈立ち。	【手の動作】 右拳はそのまま。左腕を伸ばし中高一本拳を上から振り下ろし右拳の上に重ねる。 【足の動作】 立ち方はそのまま。	【手の動作】 左中高一本拳中段打ち落とし。右拳はそのまま。 【足の動作】 立ち方はそのまま。 【留意点】 挙動19～20は連続する。

【Hands】 Slightly extend the right arm and swing right Naka-Daka-Ippon-Ken down from above (Kou is up). 【Feet】 Get ready to lower the right foot to the west.	【Hands】 Execute a Chudan-Uchi-Otoshi with right Naka-Daka-Ippon-Ken. Left fist is pulled to the left hip. 【Feet】 Right-Zenkutsudachi.	【Hands】 Keep the right fist is place. Extend the left arm and swing the left Naka-Daka-Ippon-Ken down from above and over right fist 【Feet】 Same as in ㊷.	【Hands】 Execute a Chudan-Uchi-Otoshi with left Naka-Daka-Ippon-Ken. Keep the right fist is place. 【Feet】 Same as in ㊷. 【Note】 ㊷ to ㊹ are continuous.

中高一本拳
Naka-Daka-Ippon-Ken

【手の動作】
右手は人差し指と中指を伸ばし左脇腹へ。左拳はそのまま。

【足の動作】
立ち方はそのまま。

【手の動作】
二本貫手右中段外受け。左拳は左腰に引く。

【足の動作】
立ち方はそのままで腰を左転する。

【手の動作】
左手は人差し指と中指を伸ばし眼を攻撃。右手は握りながら右腰に。

【足の動作】
右脚を軸に左足を西へすり出す。

【手の動作】
左二本貫手上段揚げ突き（軽く弧を描く）。右拳は右腰に引く。

【足の動作】
左前屈立ち。

【Hands】
Extend the right hand's index and middle fingers toward the left side (near the armpit). Keep the left fist is place.

【Feet】
Same as in ㊷.

【Hands】
Execute a Right-Chudan-Soto-Uke with Nihon-Nukite. Pull the left fist to the left hip.

【Feet】
While standing the same way, turn the hips to the left.

【Hands】
With the left hand index and middle fingers strike towards the opponent's eyes. Pull to the right hip while holding the right hand.

【Feet】
Using the right leg as the axis, slide the left leg out to the west.

【Hands】
Execute a Jodan-Age-Zuki with left Nihon-Nukite (lightly arched). Pull the right fist to the right hip.

【Feet】
Left-Zenkutsudachi.

二本貫手
Nihon-Nukite

【手の動作】
右拳は左肩前、左手は人差し指と中指を伸ばし右脇腹に持っていく。

【足の動作】
右脚を軸に体を左に回転し、左足を東へすり出す。

【手の動作】
二本貫手左中段外受け。右拳は右腰に引く。

【足の動作】
左前屈立ち。

【手の動作】
右手は人差し指と中指を伸ばし眼を攻撃。左手は握りながら左腰に。

【足の動作】
左脚を軸に右足を東へすり出す。

【手の動作】
右二本貫手上段揚げ突き（軽く弧を描く）。左拳は左腰に引く。

【足の動作】
右前屈立ち。

【Hands】
Extend the right hand's index and middle fingers toward the left side (near the armpit). Keep the left fist is place.

【Feet】
Rotate the body to the left around the right leg as the axis and slide the left leg out to the east.

【Hands】
Execute a Left-Chudan-Soto-Uke with Nihon-Nukite. Pull the right fist to the right hip.

【Feet】
Left-Zenkutsudachi.

【Hands】
With the right hand index and middle fingers strike towards the opponent's eyes. Pull to the left hip while holding the left hand.

【Feet】
Using the left leg as the axis, slide the rightt leg out to the east.

【Hands】
Execute a Jodan-Age-Zuki with right Nihon-Nukite (lightly arched). Pull the left fist to the left hip.

【Feet】
Right-Zenkutsudachi.

相手の中段突きを右掌底で受け、続いて左掌底で肘関節を打つ。さらに相手の手首をつかみ、斜め後ろに引き払う。

Deflect the opponent's Chudan-Zuki with the right Shotei, then with the left Shotei strike the elbow joint. Then grab the opponents wrist and pull it diagonally backwards.

挙動 25

【手の動作】
右掌底中段横受け。左拳はそのまま。

【足の動作】
左脚を軸として右足を北へすり出し、右足前不動立ち。

【Hands】
Execute a Right-Shotei-Chudan-Yoko-Uke. Keep the left fist is place.

【Feet】
Using the left leg as the axis, slide the right leg out to the north into a Right-Fudodachi.

挙動 26

【手の動作】
右手はそのままにして、左掌底中段外回し打ち。

【足の動作】
立ち方はそのまま。

【留意点】
左掌底は強く当てる。
挙動 25 ～ 26 は連続する。

【Hands】
Keep the right hand in place. Execute a Chudan-Soto-Mawashi-Uchi with left Shotei.

【Feet】
Same as in ⑤.

【Note】
Strike forcefully towards the left Shotei.
⑤ and ⑤ are continuous.

挙動 27

【手の動作】
両掌を握り、両側の下段へ引き払う。

【足の動作】
立ち方はそのまま。

【Hands】
Clench both hands into fists and pull away each arm to its respective side in a downward deflecting/blocking motion.

【Feet】
Same as in ⑤.

挙動 28

【手の動作】
両拳中段はさみ突き。

【足の動作】
右脚を軸に腰を左転して南へ向きを変え、やや低めの左足前不動立ち。

【留意点】
気合い。挙動 27 ～ 28 は連続する。

【Hands】
Execute a Cudan-Hasami-Zuki with both fists.

【Feet】
Turning left at the hips on the right leg as the axis, turn to the south, into left Fudodachi a little low.

【Note】
Kiai
⑤ and ⑤ are continuous.

【手の動作】
左拳を右肩前に出すとともに、右掌を左脇下からゆっくり大きく弧を描き前に出す。

【足の動作】
右足を南へすり出す。

【留意点】
右足、右手を同時にゆっくり動かす。

【手の動作】
右中段縦手刀受け。左拳は左腰に引く。

【足の動作】
右足前不動立ち。

【手の動作】
右掌に左中段縦突き。

【足の動作】
右前屈立ち。

【手の動作】
右拳を左肩前に出すとともに、左掌を右脇下からゆっくり大きく弧を描き前に出す。

【足の動作】
左足を南へすり出す。

【留意点】
左足、左手を同時にゆっくり動かす。

【Hands】
Extend left fist in front of right shoulder, and draw out a large arc from below the left armpit to the front with open right hand.

【Feet】
Slide the right foot to the south.

【Note】
Right foot and right hand move slowly and simultaneously.

【Hands】
Execute a Right-Chudan-Tate-Shuto-Uke. Pull back left fist to the left hip.

【Feet】
Right-Fudodachi.

【Hands】
Execute a Left Chudan-Tate-Zuki to the right palm.

【Feet】
Right-Zenkutsudachi.

【Hands】
Extend the right fist in front of the left shoulder, and draw out a large arc from below the right armpit to the front with open left hand.

【Feet】
Slide the left foot to the south.

【Note】
Left foot and left hand move slowly and simultaneously.

| 挙動31 | 挙動32 | 途中 | 途中 |

61　62　63　64

【手の動作】
左中段縦手刀受け。右拳は右腰に引く。

【足の動作】
左足前不動立ち。

【手の動作】
左掌に右中段縦突き。

【足の動作】
左前屈立ち。

【手の動作】
右拳を左掌で包み、両肘を軽く曲げ、両拳を胸前に引き寄せる。

【足の動作】
左足を右足に引き寄せる。

【手の動作】
両手はそのまま。

【足の動作】
閉足立ち。

【留意点】
閉足立ちになると同時にすり足で一歩下がる。

【Hands】
Execute a Left-Chudan-Tate-Shuto-Uke. Pull back right fist to the right hip.

【Feet】
Left-Fudodachi.

【Note】
Do slowly.

【Hands】
Execute a Right Chudan-Tate-Zuki to the left palm.

【Feet】
Left-Zenkutsudachi.

【Hands】
Wrap the right fist the left the palm, bend both elbows slightly, and pull both fists in front of the chest.

【Feet】
Pull the left foot back alongside the right foot.

【Hands】
Same as in ⑥③.

【Feet】
Heisokudachi.

【Note】
Simultaneously as a Heisokudachi, take a step back with a Suriashi.

| 途中 | 途中 | 止め | 直立 |

65　　　　　　　66　　　　　　　67　　　　　　　68

【手の動作】
両手はそのまま。

【足の動作】
閉足立ち。

【留意点】
続けてすり足で一歩下がる。

【手の動作】
両手はそのまま。

【足の動作】
閉足立ち。

【留意点】
さらにかるくはずみをつけてすり足で一歩下がる。

【手の動作】
両手はそのまま。

【足の動作】
閉足立ち。

【手の動作】
両手は開いて大腿部両側に付けて伸ばす。

【足の動作】
結び立ち。

【Hands】
Same as in ㉚.

【Feet】
Heisokudachi.

【Note】
Continue by sliding one step back.

【Hands】
Same as in ㉚.

【Feet】
Heisokudachi.

【Note】
Bounce lightly/gently back one step.

【Hands】
Same as in ㉚.

【Feet】
Heisokudachi.

【Hands】
Open both hands and extend them down along the sides of the thighs.

【Feet】
Musubidachi.

| 礼 | 直立 |

礼をする。

【手の動作】
手はそのまま。

【足の動作】
足はそのまま。

* Bow (Rei).

【Hands】
Same as in 69.

【Feet】
Same as in 69.

監修

（一財）全日本空手道松涛館　中央技術委員会
　　　津山捷泰　　　Tsuyama Katsuhiro
　　　阪梨　學　　　Sakanashi Manabu
　　　香川政夫　　　Kagawa Masao
　　　香川政義　　　Kagawa Masayoshi
　　　粕谷文男　　　Kasuya Fumio
　　　小松幸司　　　Komatsu Koji
　　　森田賢次　　　Morita Kenji

■編集協力
　　　伊志嶺実　　　Ishimine Minoru
　　　松江　肇　　　Matsue Hajime

■演武協力
　　　在本幸司　　　Arimoto Koji

■翻訳協力
　　　Kyle Kamal Helou
　　　空手道マガジンJKFan編集部

松涛館流空手道形教範全集　得意形Ⅲ　鉄騎二段・鉄騎三段・半月・十手・珍手

2024年9月14日発行

編集　　一般財団法人全日本空手道松涛館　中央技術委員会
編者　　一般財団法人全日本空手道松涛館
発行　　株式会社チャンプ
　　　　〒166-0003　東京都杉並区高円寺南4-19-3　総和第二ビル
　　　　電話：03-3315-3190（営業部）

©ALL Japan Karatedo Shotokan 2024
Printed in Japan　印刷：シナノ印刷株式会社

定価はカバーに表示してあります。
乱丁・落丁本は、ご面倒ですが、(株)チャンプ宛にご送付ください。送料小社負担にてお取り替えいたします。

ISBN978-4-86344-029-6